THE GREATEST FOOTBALLER ENGLAND NEVER HAD
THE KEVIN BEATTIE STORY

AS TOLD TO ROB FINCH

www.cultfigurepublishing.com

Find out more about Cult Figure Publishing and future titles at:
www.cultfigurepublishing.com

Typesetting by INVENTIVE RECEPTION in Garamond 12/16pt.
Printed by Colchester Print Group.

ISBN-13 978-0-9554884-0-5

CONTENTS

ACKNOWLEDGEMENTS

Rob Finch and Kevin Beattie would like to thank the following people for their support in helping produce this book: David Allard, Julie Armstrong, Terry Baxter, Mike Buck, Maggie Beattie, Michael Finch, Duncan Foster at Framlingham Properties and Omnicorp, Matthew Galvin at Inventive Reception, Anthony Grunberg, Mel Henderson, Faz Mandini, Bob Shelley.

***

Kevin Beattie was born in Carlisle in 1953. He was the inaugural PFA Young Footballer of the Year and was awarded international recognition by England. He was tipped to win over 100 caps, however his career was cut short due to a succession of injuries. For this reason he is seen as the great lost talent of English football. Today he lives quietly with his family in Ipswich.

Rob Finch is an avid sports fan and a freelance writer and publisher from Beverley, East Yorkshire. He worked closely with Kevin on this story. Rob is working on several other book titles at the moment. Keep checking www.cultfigurepublishing.com for details.

Every effort was made to contact relevant photograph copyright holders.

FOREWORD BY
SIR BOBBY ROBSON CBE

As a football player for England, I was blessed to have lined up alongside some of the great names in the history of the game. I witnessed first hand the delightful artistry of Tom Finney and the majesty of Bobby Charlton whose surging forward runs and explosive shooting ability remains unsurpassed. At the back was the wonderfully consistent Billy Wright and alongside him was the sublime Duncan Edwards, who was so cruelly taken from us when not even in his prime.

When I was later fortunate enough to become the England team manager, I was also lucky enough to have some wonderful footballers at my disposal. The tenacious box to box style of play demonstrated by Bryan Robson was a brand of football many years before its time. I watched the impish trickery of Paul Gascoigne so nearly take us to World Cup glory. I also saw the goal-scoring prowess of ace marksman Gary Lineker, a man who ruthlessly punished any defensive errors in or around the six-yard box.

When you add a certain Alan Shearer to the list – who I of course managed at Newcastle United, then I think I am better qualified than most to pass judgement on the great English born football players who have played the game. As illustrious a list as that is, for me there is one player who is better than all of those named above and I do not make that statement lightly.

I would say that in my opinion, he is without doubt the best English born player I have witnessed during my fifty odd year association with the game and his name is Kevin Beattie. He arrived at Portman Road, at fifteen years of age with nothing – literally a brown paper bag with an old pair of football boots inside. Although he may have possessed nothing, Kevin was blessed with everything.

His was a God-given talent and I don't really think that Kevin ever truly appreciated what a great player he was. He was born a magnificent athlete, with a fantastic rippling physique and he possessed every attribute a footballer needs. He could climb higher than the crossbar and still head the ball downwards. He had the sweetest left-foot that I have ever seen and without even looking, could hit sixty-yard passes, that would eliminate six opposition players from the game.

He had strength, was lightning quick and he could tackle. He was a superb defender, but also magnificent going forward. He was versatile and could play anywhere on the park, he was also brave, maybe too brave at times, but I was so grateful that he was on my side, for as a player I would have hated to play against him.

As a man Kevin was great to be with and was great to have around and whilst I sometimes labelled him 'daft as a brush,' there isn't an ounce of malice in his body. It was a tragedy when Kevin had to finish due to his ongoing injury problems and he was a great loss to both Ipswich Town and especially England as he should have won over a hundred caps and not the nine that he eventually did.

I know that since quitting football, he has had his problems

away from the game, however with typical tenacity he is still
around and still battling. It is a pleasure to write the foreword to
Kevin's book, he was an imperious footballer and is also a lovely
man. I wish him every success as it was a pleasure and a privilege
to be his manager.

Sir Bobby Robson CBE

THE GREATEST FOOTBALLER ENGLAND NEVER HAD
THE KEVIN BEATTIE STORY

PRE-MATCH

Put me on a football pitch and stick a number six shirt on my back and life was very easy. From being a young player of sixteen years of age, I was compared to the great Duncan Edwards and seen as the natural heir to Bobby Moore. Like the great man, it was also assumed that I would be the captain of England and win over 100 caps.

Shortly after I had finished playing, Bobby told me that when he first saw me play, he thought I would win more caps than he did and he won an incredible total of 108. He was a legend and a lovely man to boot, so to hear those words was something special. Over the years, the compliments flowed from the lips of the great and the good. Sir Alf Ramsey, Sir Bobby Robson, Sir Bobby Charlton, Don Revie, Bill Shankly, Brian Clough – they all told me that I was an incredible player and spoke in glowing terms about me and those were fellows who knew their football.

Unfortunately it doesn't always work out how you imagine and my life has been less than straightforward. I have had my share of misfortune and also made some bad decisions. Throw in some devastating injuries which have left me with mobility problems to this day and it may explain why I might be described as the best player England never had.

I've heard people say I would be worth a record fee if I played now and my old boss Sir Bobby Robson has said that from 1972 to 1978, I would have walked into any side in the game. It is very flattering, but also somewhat ironic as I felt the best was yet to come.

That it didn't go as planned doesn't mean that I am looking for sympathy or providing excuses. Nor am I wallowing in self-pity as despite my bad luck, I still feel that I have been blessed. I'm also very proud to have represented my country and to have played for a club as wonderful as Ipswich Town, where I enjoyed some terrific times.

It's very trite to say I would have played the game for nothing, but I would and I never could get used to being paid to do something that I adored. For a large chunk of my career I played in pain and carried on when others would have refused to cross the white line. I want no compliments for that, it is just the way I am, I wanted to play the game I love, the game I was born to play.

I was born on December 18th 1953 in Carlisle, Cumbria, it is said that there is a curse on the city, one which was cast by Archbishop Dunbar of Glasgow in 1525. It has supposedly afflicted both Carlisle and its inhabitants ever since and natural disasters such as the terrible floods which have plagued the area and the lack of progress made by Carlisle United, are examples of things which are often put down to the dreaded curse.

As a native of the city, it has often been suggested that I am also a victim. Indeed my old boss, Sir Bobby Robson, has stated on many occasions that I was equally blessed and cursed. Blessed with great natural football ability and cursed by a succession of injuries and misfortune, that not only ended my football career but plagued me in life beyond the game.

I was christened Thomas Beattie, though I soon dropped the Thomas part and used my middle name of Kevin, as my Dad was also called Thomas Beattie. I had got sick of answering calls for 'Tommy' only to find that it was my Dad somebody wanted to see and not me. My Dad was also a renowned hard-man, with a bit of a reputation on the estate where I lived and so carving out a separate name, as well as a separate identity was important to me.

My Grandmother's maiden name was Tudor and it is rumoured that she was a descendent of the famous Tudor dynasty, which at one time ruled the land. Whilst my blue-blooded ancestors would have lived in grand palaces and country mansions, my own upbringing was held in very different circumstances. I can't think of too many members of the Royal family who were brought up in a council house in Carlisle, but it was here that I spent my formative years.

My home was based in Botcherby, which is a large estate in the city and as part of what was once a frontier town, it certainly had its fair share of characters and hard-cases. People did not stand on ceremony and they told it as they saw it and it was certainly a rough and tumble affair that's for sure. My parents always did the best that they could, but we didn't have much, in fact it's fair to say we didn't have anything. However, nor did too many other people on the estate, so I never felt too left out and I never felt inferior. When everybody else you come into contact with has nothing, you don't really feel that you are missing out.

My Dad worked for the national coal board, delivering coal and my Mum worked as a cleaner in a shop for the Lipton tea company. Neither of them earned very good wages, so money was always an issue. Eventually my Dad had to pack in work altogether due to a back complaint and tough times subsequently became even tougher.

It became especially difficult for my Mum, as she was now not only the solitary wage earner in the family, she also had to continue with her responsibilities of looking after the family and keeping the house clean and tidy. In many ways, she was left with an impossible job, although she always did her best. She was a lovely woman who had a very tough life and she deserved a better fate, although I never heard her complain about things and she always had a smile on her face.

My Dad was a great man when he was sober, when he would be kind and thoughtful. He was a real character and always up for a laugh and a joke. However when he had been drinking, he was a different animal altogether. He would want to take on everyone and as a well known local hard-man he wasn't a fellow to tangle with. There were a few people on the estate that tried their luck with him and regretted it and I can also remember getting a clip round the ear for my troubles when I stepped out of line. Unfortunately for me, his hands were big – literally the size of a shovel, so when I did get a clump it wasn't one ear that felt the force, but both of them. His hands were so big that they literally extended from one side of my head to the other.

As a man he didn't handle responsibility well and especially after he lost his job, he found solace in a drink. If he had money in his pocket, which was rare, he would be straight down to the local pub. As a result my Mum was left to make ends meet and feed a family of ten, as I also had four brothers and four sisters.

The food for the week would be bought on a Friday but by the following Monday or Tuesday it was invariably gone. For the rest of the week, there was often only food on the table when my Dad had backed a winning horse, or else won a game of darts, or dominoes down at his local pub. I remember eagerly waiting for him to come home from the pub and if he had won, there would be a fish supper tucked under his arm, though if he'd lost there would be nothing.

With an empty stomach to fill, I often took to raiding the local allotments for fruit and vegetables and would bring something back for my Mum to cook. She would ask where it had come from and I would tell her that it had been given to me. I'm not sure she always believed me but with nothing in the cupboards, she wasn't in a position to query things too much.

I was also fortunate in that I had two good pals at the time, whose families ran a fish and chip shop and an ice-cream parlour respectively. Their parents took something of a shine to me and if I hadn't eaten anything that day then they would make sure that I didn't go hungry.

We lived in a three-bedroom house and with so many of us in the family I shared not just a bedroom but a bed. It wasn't ideal and was even worse during the winter months. Living so far north meant that it would get unbearably cold and Mum and Dad would have to throw coats over the bed to help keep us warm. Though during one particularly bad winter, we were still freezing cold, so my Dad had to take drastic action.

He couldn't afford to pay the bills and as he wasn't prepared to see his family going cold, he managed to fix the electricity meter so that we got a free supply. It was fine for a while, however the electricity board soon found out and the police were called. My Dad was no stranger to trouble with the law, however this was more serious than his previous encounters, which had been for the odd pub dust-up and he was immediately arrested and remanded in custody.

The authorities seemed to be sending out the message that they wouldn't tolerate this kind of thing, as a few weeks later after appearing in court, he was sentenced to three months in Durham prison. My Mum was at her wits end and it was a very traumatic time for her, although as a youngster I was oblivious to it all. In all honesty, my Dad was never the type of fellow to be at home with the proverbial pipe and slippers and so his absence wasn't even that noticeable to me.

I can remember going with my Mum for a day out to see him and as it was the first time I had been away from Carlisle, I treated it as a great adventure and something of a day out. I got dressed up and as we travelled across the country to Durham, I can remember feeling quite excited by the whole thing. It was as if we were heading out for a day at the seaside, rather than to a maximum security prison and never once did I feel intimidated or bad about where I was going.

When we arrived, it was good to see my Dad as he hadn't been able to get access to alcohol and he was back to displaying the kind and generous side of his nature that I loved. He was very attentive and really pleased to see me, which was something that I really enjoyed as when he had been drinking he would sometimes be very difficult and irritable. The whole day was a great success and I wanted to go back again as soon as possible. It sounds bizarre when you consider the circumstances of the visit, but I can even remember posing for photographs against the backdrop of the Durham skyline, where you could clearly see the prison in the background.

Although the visit to the prison hadn't been at all traumatic, or cause for any sense of shame within the family, it certainly provoked a response from some of the neighbours. It was somewhat ironic, as my Dad wasn't the first and certainly wouldn't be the last person from the estate to go to prison. However the story had made a big splash in the local newspapers and so everyone in the area knew what had happened.

Eventually some of the local kids started to make sarcastic remarks. I didn't like what I heard and I found myself involved in a few fights over it all. It soon made me question my feelings about my Dad's situation, as I was like most youngsters in that I didn't like to be seen to be different. Although deep-down, I couldn't really see anything to feel embarrassed about. As far as I could see, all my Dad had done was help his family and I didn't see anything wrong with that.

Despite the tough surroundings, I had a fairly contented childhood, although the atmosphere at home was not always the greatest. With money being so tight and my Dad often spending what bit he had down at the pub, arguments were never too far away. I can remember my Mum and Dad having some blazing rows, although they always made up soon afterwards.

Despite my Dad's irresponsible behaviour my parents were actually a very devoted couple, who were very much in love. They certainly had their trials and tribulations but they were to remain married for over thirty years and were only parted when my Dad eventually passed away in 1983.

As my Dad was often down at the pub, I was curious as to what the attraction was. I had visions of it being a magical place and assumed it must be a wonderful environment to be, as not only my Dad, but a large proportion of other people on the estate wanted to be there all the time. I obviously couldn't get into the pub, but I remember when I was about ten or eleven years old getting him to bring back some booze, so that I could taste what it was like.

Although I developed a taste for it in later life, at that time I didn't like it and thought it was disgusting and I couldn't understand how anyone could drink so much as a mouthful, let alone pint after pint of the stuff. Around the same time, I started having a crafty smoke and unlike the drink, developed an immediate liking for it. I soon began needing a regular fix of nicotine and I was soon puffing my way through a packet of cigarettes a day. Unfortunately a habit I kept up throughout my playing career and one which I have maintained to this day.

I actually thought by having a drink or a smoke it might make me appear more of a man and create a better situation between myself and my Dad. I really wanted to earn his respect as unlike a lot of other father/son relationships, we did very little together. Obviously I was going the wrong way about it and with hindsight it was a ridiculous notion. However I was young and confused as to why my relationship was somewhat different to the relationship I saw other lads having with their own Dad. So in order to try and rectify this, I decided to take drastic action.

My Dad had a tattoo of a woman on his forearm and I used to love to see it, as when he flexed his burly arm the woman appeared to 'dance.' My Dad also seemed to enjoy showing it off and so the tattoo became something that brought us together. Thinking it would help us bond further, I wanted to get a tattoo of my own. I was ten years old and had no money, so I got a darning needle and some ink and set to work. It was incredibly painful as I repeatedly jabbed the needle into my arm, but eventually I had my tattoo. At the time I had a schoolboy crush on a girl called Sue and so my tattoo was done in her honour and her name still adorns my forearm today.

I rushed home to show my Dad and expected him to be pleased. Of course he was less than thrilled that his ten-year old son now had the word 'Sue' scrawled on his arm. We did bond, and there was something of a 'coming together' moment, but not in the way I had wanted. Unfortunately for me, it entailed his shovel-like hand lamping me around the ear and packing me off to bed.

It was a hard lesson learned, but that was nothing new for me. My formal education was at St Cuthbert's RC school in Carlisle, but I learned my most important lessons on the streets around my home. They were home to several gangs and if you strayed into rival territory, you would get beaten-up for your troubles.

The playing-fields near to where I lived were often the scene of a pitched battle between opposing factions and if you didn't learn how to fight, then you would soon become an easy target. Like most lads of my age I got into my share of scrapes and had to learn the hard way how to survive. Fortunately I was a fairly big lad, with an athletic build and I could more than hold my own. Although later, when it escalated from fist fights into battles with sticks, weapons and the like, I did my best to keep out of the way, which was sometimes easier said than done.

Despite my best efforts, trouble – as is often the case, came looking for me. My parents couldn't afford to buy me long trousers and I remember that because of this, the school bully picked me out and started giving me a hard time. I tried to ignore him and of course he wasn't happy with that, so he began hitting my bare legs with a piece of branch that he'd ripped from a tree.

I wasn't having that, so I hit him and like most bullies, he didn't want to know when someone stood up to him. Word soon got out as to what had happened and people were keen to leave me alone after that. It certainly toughened me up and I learned how important it was to stand your ground and not let anyone push you about.

It was an attitude that I took to the local playing fields where I learned how to play football. They were the scene of the traditional, 'jumpers for goalposts' games that would go long into the night. Playing twenty-plus per side on bumpy pitches, dodging dog shit and pot-holes wouldn't be seen in too many coaching manuals and rightly so, but it was here that I was able to hone my skills and learn my craft as a footballer. The games often featured older lads and even grown men and nobody was worried about clattering into you in order to put you out of your stride. I soon learned that not only did I have to play hard, I also had to play smart and use a bit of guile and cunning to deal with guys who were much bigger and stronger than I was at the time.

I was at this point attending the St Cuthbert junior school and was asked to become a member of the school football eleven. The only problem was that I couldn't afford any boots, which was a pre-requisite of being allowed to play. I thought that it had ruined my chances, when a fantastic teacher I had called Mr Rafferty went out and bought me some with his own money. In many ways I would credit him with first developing my interest in the game.

On my first day at school aged five, like many kids I screamed the place down as soon as my Mum left me at the school gates. In order to try and calm me down, Mr Rafferty came over and gave me a football and it did the trick. I was no longer worried about my Mum or being in a strange environment, instead I was fascinated by everything to do with football and my love affair with the game had commenced.

Mr Rafferty had also unwittingly helped with my attendance at school, as I was to associate going there with football. It was important as I can't say that I was too inspired by what else was on offer and so if it hadn't been for football, I doubt that I would have gone back. Not only was Mr Rafferty a lovely man, he was also a tremendous teacher, who inspired everyone around him and filled them with confidence. I was a bit reserved in those days and Mr Rafferty helped improve my self-esteem, which is of course very important to anyone, particularly a footballer, as all of the great players have that little swagger in their step. Looking back, most of the pupils at the school didn't have much going for them or have too many role-models to aspire to. I know I didn't and so Mr Rafferty became a very instrumental figure in my early life.

I was actually a goal-keeper in those early days and as well as my local team Carlisle United, I also had a soft spot for Chelsea. The reason that I picked them out was because the team seemed a very exciting one and it also seemed a glamorous place, which was the opposite of where I lived in the north of England.

Like most young lads, I would fantasise that I was a famous player whenever I was playing and I always used to imagine that I was Peter Bonetti, the Chelsea goal-keeper known as 'the Cat.' My Dad had also played in that position and had put those big hands of his to good use, so much so, that he once had trials with Aston Villa, although he never followed it up, as the money they were offering him was worse than the wages he earned from the coal board.

It was for that reason I gravitated to a role between the posts, however with Mr Rafferty's advice, I soon began playing outfield, although I played as a striker, rather than as a defender where I made my name as a professional player. My new hero became Peter Osgood and I used to try and copy him. I picked up some useful tips and as I was also very quick and could beat anyone for pace, I scored an average of two goals per game whilst at the school.

Although we were a fairly small school, with not too many players to pick from, Mr Rafferty soon turned us into a well drilled outfit and we went a full season undefeated. We then met our local rivals in the cup final, although it was a game too far and we lost the match 3-2. It was eventually time to leave St Cuthbert's and whilst I was never the most enthusiastic of scholars, I passed my eleven plus and was set for a place at the local grammar school. However I soon had a dilemma, as all the lads who I knew from Botcherby at the time, had failed the exam and were going to the local comprehensive.

I was torn between accepting the chance of a better education or staying with my mates and for a while didn't know what to do. In the end my mind was made up for me when my parents told me they couldn't afford the grammar school uniform, which was a fancy affair, comprising of a blazer, pleated trousers and the like. When I later found out the grammar school concentrated more on rugby-union than playing football, I certainly had no regrets about it all.

My new school was called St Patrick's RC senior school, although I had very little interest in the place. The only thing I cared about was football and I soon got into the school side, I also played in a local amateur boy's team managed by my old teacher Mr Rafferty called Blackfriars. It was good to maintain the relationship with him and I continued to listen and learn. It was here that people were beginning to take notice of me and after games I started to hear one or two parents saying nice things about me and telling me that I looked like a genuine prospect. As any young lad who plays football will tell you, there is nothing better than a grown-up, who has been around and obviously seen a lot of football telling you that you can play the game.

I was really encouraged by it all and like most lads, I soon harboured dreams about making it as a professional player, although it seemed that things like that happened to other people and not someone from the backstreets of Botcherby. It also didn't help my confidence that my Dad never bothered to come to see any games, which I was always sad about as I wanted to make him feel proud of me.

In many ways it was a good job I was doing well on the football pitch, as my academic career left a bit to be desired. I was never a disruptive or disrespectful pupil, I just wasn't that interested. I was a normal 'lad' and got into the usual scrapes, but I was never a tearaway. I think the worst thing that I did was when I used to go smoking with a group of lads behind the school boiler.

We used to take it in turns to keep guard and one day we put a lad there who was a bit of a nervous type. We didn't know that when he got edgy, he started stuttering, so there we were puffing away like chimneys when we got a tap on the shoulder from one of the teachers. Stood beside him, shaking like a leaf, was the lad who was still trying to get his words of warning out. All harmless enough stuff I suppose, but hardly likely to win me any awards on the school prize giving day.

In truth, I was rarely if ever there, as I used to bunk off with my mates and we'd go kick a football about. When I did roll into school, it was only because there was a PE lesson or a game of football on the go. I used to forge notes from my Dad saying that I had been ill and I have no doubt that the teachers knew what was going on, but I was an asset to the school football team, so nothing much was said. I was left alone and allowed to enjoy my football, as I think they knew that I wasn't the type to pay too much attention to what was been said in any of the other lessons anyway.

If the school weren't so bothered about my continued absence, then unfortunately the local authorities were. After several warnings from the school inspector, I received a letter ordering me to go to court to explain my lack of attendance at school. Fortunately by the time my appearance before the magistrates arrived, I was becoming known as an exciting football prospect. I think the magistrates realised that I wasn't a bad lad and didn't want to mess up my chances of making it as a football player, so with that, I was given a warning and sent on my way.

Whilst I wasn't the most enthusiastic, or natural of students, it was quite the opposite situation on the sports field. Not only was I doing well on the football pitch, I was also the school sprint champion, although it was 100 yards rather than metres in those days. I was able to cover that distance – some 91.44 metres, in approximately ten seconds dead. This was in my football boots which I used as I couldn't afford proper running spikes.

By the time I was fourteen, I had also started playing for a pub team called The Magpie, who played in the local league, I continued to play up-front, whilst my Dad played in goal. It was nice to be lining up alongside him, as we finally began doing something together. It was also reassuring, as I was playing against grown men who did not stand on ceremony. Although it was good for my continuing football education and I learned a lot in a short space of time. You had to as you would not have survived – simple as that.

My progress was rapid and I soon heard that Celtic had shown an interest in me, but somebody had mistakenly told them that I was not a Catholic and that seemed to cool their interest. Mr Rafferty also spoke to Carlisle United about taking me on, but at that time they had no junior side, so that was the end of that. It did seem like my dream of becoming a professional footballer was a far-fetched notion and at this point places like Brunton Park never mind Stamford Bridge and Old Trafford seemed a million miles away.

Being a local lad I was of course an ardent Carlisle United fan and I was devastated when I heard the news that they had no junior side. I would have loved to have played for the club, especially as I couldn't afford to see too many games. Although I always scoured the newspapers for the match reports and often hung around Brunton Park just to soak up the atmosphere or catch an autograph or two.

One of my heroes at the time, was the club's star striker Hughie McIlmoyle who once scored 42 goals in a single season for the club. I remember joining a group of other fans after one game in the pouring rain, in the hope that I could get his signature. After hanging around for an age, Hughie eventually emerged, but when I thrust my pen and paper in his direction, he brushed past me and brusquely told me he was in a rush. I was of course devastated and never forgot how I had felt that afternoon, when autograph hunters subsequently came my way.

Many years later when I was myself a famous footballer, I met Hughie at a Carlisle United function and I reminded him of the story. He apologised profusely and there was certainly no grudge on my part, as we got on famously and he was a very nice man. In fact we staged a photograph for the local newspaper, where I finally got my long awaited autograph and we generally had a good laugh about it all.

Although I was beginning to make something of a name for myself on the football field, I had surprisingly failed to draw the attention of the selectors of the Cumbria County schools representative side. They are an early benchmark about who is likely to make the grade and when they didn't pick me, it made me feel that I wasn't good enough. I was to later find out that they had a preference for lads who attended the grammar schools and often never bothered watching the comprehensive school teams. Although I didn't know that fact at the time, so it became a bit disheartening.

Eventually I did make a team which was put together to represent a Carlisle school select eleven, although for some reason I was never asked back again. I remember that it was an established team and it was full of lads who were all over six feet tall and looked like they had been shaving for two or three years. It didn't faze me as I was used to playing against bigger lads, but I didn't like it that the emphasis was about size rather than skill, as that's not what football should be about.

The atmosphere was also very cliquey, which wasn't what I had been used to, as all the clubs I had played for, had a set of lads who were all in it together. The overall feeling I got was one of confusion and I wasn't really bothered that they didn't ask me back. Apart from that incident, I continued to enjoy my football, whether in the park games around Botcherby, or with my Dad for the pub team, or indeed with school. Where we soon made amends for my earlier primary school cup defeat, by lifting the cup, with yours truly, still a striker at this time, netting twice. My school days were soon to end and there was never much chance of me staying on. I needed to earn some money, so as soon as I was able I left. I was just shy of my fifteenth birthday and set off to work as a machine fitter, but it was not really for me and so I soon packed it in. Over the course of the next year I tried my hand at a number of things but found it hard to settle at anything, as my head was always full of football.

Jobs came and jobs went, I was a delivery boy, worked in a few factories and also a fruit and vegetable warehouse. Although I soon packed it in there, when one day I lifted up a box of bananas and a spider as big as my hand fell on top of me. The worst job I had at this time was that of a 'chippy,' which might sound like I was involved in carpentry of some sort, but the job actually meant working in a laundry/dry-cleaners and 'chipping' (hence the name) the debris from the items that had been brought in to be cleaned.

I had to remove stubborn stains by hand before they were washed or dry cleaned, which often meant 'chipping' off things like food, but more often than not it entailed 'chipping' off human excrement as one of the best customers was a local retirement home. It was hot, stinking, mind-numbing work and after a few months I packed it in. I really couldn't stand the place and couldn't bear to think that I might spend the rest of my life there. Luckily it was a time of full employment and you were able to leave a job on a Friday, knowing full well that there were plenty of other places to start work come Monday morning.

I soon started working for a local furniture company and can say that it was the only job I enjoyed at this time. The best part was that I got to travel all over Cumbria delivering beds and furniture to customers. I really enjoyed seeing different places, as apart from a week's holiday in Blackpool with my family and the trip to Durham prison, I had never been out of Carlisle. The old guy I worked with really looked after me and was a lovely person, who often brought me some sandwiches or fruit, as I couldn't always afford to buy my own lunch. As well as that, the constant lugging of heavy items helped build up my strength and kept me in good shape.

However all I really wanted to do was play football and it was still proving hard to settle down to anything else. I was of course still playing and I turned out for a team called St Augustine on a Saturday and for Mr Rafferty at Blackfriars on a Sunday. The goals continued to flow and I scored eight in one game, which was to earn me my first mention in the local press and was a proud moment for me.

At this stage a lot of people were telling me that I was good enough to be a professional player and I began to think that I might have a chance of making it. Even so, it was a surprise when after one particular game a gentleman came over and introduced himself. He told me that he was a scout for Liverpool football club and asked me if I wanted to go down for a trial.

I was stunned but of course the answer was yes. However in those days you needed permission before you could go on trial, so as I only lived around the corner I took the scout home with me. My Mum didn't really understand what was going on and my Dad, as was becoming increasingly common was down at the pub. It was hard work getting him to leave his pint behind, but I eventually got him home. I am not sure what the scout made of it all, but after speaking to him, my Dad gave me permission to go and a trial date was set for the following week. I wasn't nervous about things and couldn't wait to get down there and get stuck in and the following week couldn't arrive quickly enough for me. Although when I made my way down to Liverpool, the reality of the situation kicked in as I was only fifteen years old and it seemed a long way to be going on my own. I was therefore relieved to be met by someone from the club at Lime Street train station.

I was taken to the home of another club apprentice, which was common practice for young players who were on trial. I was told I would be staying there for the duration of my time in Liverpool, as it obviously gave me a home away from home and put me with someone of my own age. I ended up staying at the home of Phil Thompson and we hit it off straight away. We were both desperate to make the grade and both lived for our football. Phil's family also looked after me tremendously, which I appreciated and haven't forgotten. He of course went on to have a fantastic career at Liverpool and remains a good friend to this day.

The manager at the time was of course the great Bill Shankly and I was immediately struck by the aura he had about him. He was only a small man, but literally filled the room with his presence and you could tell that he was the man in charge, as when he spoke everyone listened. I also remember seeing Tommy Smith who had already acquired a fearsome reputation in the game. In later years I got to know Tommy quite well as we had gone through similar experiences with our football related injuries and although his image is that of a tough-guy, he is in reality a very nice man.

It was in fact another Liverpool hard-man who I briefly upset whilst on trial. This came during a practice game comprising of teams made up of the younger trial players and apprentices, who played against the first-team.

A few minutes into the game, I easily beat Larry Lloyd in the air and he immediately warned me in no uncertain terms not to do it again. Larry was much bigger than me and also an established player, so I don't think he took kindly to being beaten by a young trial player. At the time I wasn't sure if he meant what he said, however I later realised that it was nothing personal and was the kind of mind games I would have to get used to if I wanted to make it as a professional player.

There were a number of other players on trial there and apart from the game we played, we remained on one side of the pitch, whilst the first team players such as Tommy, Larry and Ian St John, were kept away from us on the other side of the ground. I did feel a bit left out by this as I thought we would all be playing together. However I think it was a psychological thing and a means of separating those that had made the grade, from those that merely wanted to.

I didn't let it affect my game though and I must have done well as Mr Shankly told me he was very impressed and that he would like me to sign for the club on a full-time basis. He asked me to come back the following week to spend some more time at the club and to sort out a contract. It was an amazing moment, as only a few weeks earlier I had been playing on the park pitches around Carlisle and working in a succession of dead-end jobs and here I was being courted by the great Bill Shankly and Liverpool football club. Most of the people back home couldn't believe the news and it seemed like my life was about to change in the most dramatic way.

The following week I arrived at Liverpool's Lime Street station and was again expecting to be met by one of the club officials, only to find there was no one there. I was as green as grass in those days and so genuinely didn't know what to do. I had still not turned sixteen years of age and had barely been outside of Carlisle. I was in a strange city and unsure of where to go and certainly didn't have the sense to get myself across the city to the training ground.

I literally only had my football boots and a train ticket (which Liverpool had paid for) to my name and didn't have the price of a bus fare, let alone a taxi to help me on my way. An old ticket collector at the station obviously realised something was wrong and came over to ask if he could help. I explained my predicament and as a Liverpool fan he soon took an interest. He told me that he had often seen various officials from the club at the station picking up players and the like. Although as far as he was aware, no one had been there that day.

As I was wondering what to do next, the next train heading to Carlisle pulled in, I assumed Liverpool had changed their mind and not wishing to spend a night in the city on my own, I hopped on the train and headed home. Looking back it was a crazy decision to have taken, however I was very unworldly and really didn't know what to do. With hindsight I should obviously have made contact with the club and found out what was going on, however when you are fifteen years old and in a strange city, with no money in your pocket, it's more difficult to act in a confident, experienced and self-assured manner.

It was a long journey home and I was in a real state emotionally as I couldn't work out what had happened. To make matters worse, when I arrived home I had to trudge several miles across Carlisle in the pouring rain. I felt really let down, as I was a kid from the back streets, who had been offered a great opportunity only to seemingly have it taken away again. I had often thought that making it as a footballer happened to other lads and not the likes of me and this situation seemed to confirm what I always really thought.

My Dad was astounded when I arrived home and he assumed I had done something wrong and had been kicked out by the club, or had simply not turned up. He began giving me the third degree, however, I had the foresight to get my ticket stamped at the station, to prove that I had made the journey to Liverpool and he began to back off. He was no longer annoyed at me and began venting his anger at the football club. It was a good job that no-one from the club was there at that time as they might well have felt the force of one of those big hands my Dad possessed.

A couple of days later and still feeling devastated by what had happened, I received a letter with a Liverpool post mark on it. It could only be from the club, so I eagerly ripped it open. I was hoping that inside was another invitation to come down and an explanation as to what had gone wrong. Instead I received a very brief two-lined note, which told me that they were no longer interested in my services as I had 'Failed to turn up.'

It seemed that the dream was over and I was stuck in Botcherby forever and that my football would be limited to a game on a weekend for some local side and that I would have to earn my living from one of the dead-end jobs that had been my stock and trade up until that point. I was also devastated that the club would think such a thing, as why on earth would I not want to turn up to play for the great Liverpool football club?

KICK-OFF

I was about to get in touch with the club and explain my side of the story, when a couple of days later I was approached by another scout called John Carruthers, who told me that he represented Ipswich Town. He said that he had heard extremely good reports about me and that he would like me to go there for a trial. I hadn't even heard of the place, let alone the football club and following the disappointment of my Liverpool experience, I was feeling a little confused by things. I wasn't sure what to do about Liverpool, but I assumed that when a person like Bill Shankly makes a decision, he wouldn't be the type to change his mind.

I therefore decided to forget about Liverpool and give things a go at Ipswich, I was desperate to make the grade and so I was soon on my way south. I had been told to report to Euston station in London, as I was playing in a youth-team game against Fulham. It was the furthest I had ever being away from home and it was a long and tiring journey.

As I made my way across the station platform following my arrival, I began to panic as I feared another Liverpool scenario. I was also nervous as I desperately wanted it to work out. I had nothing going for me in life and I didn't want to be stuck in a dead-end job forever. I knew that my only route out was through football and I was determined to make things work.

As had happened at Liverpool, I arrived with nothing except a train ticket and my football boots. All I owned in life was the clothes I was standing in and the truth of the matter was that I didn't even own all of those. I was actually wearing my Dad's shoes as I didn't have a decent pair of my own. However I needn't have worried. I was met by the chief- scout at the time, a bear of a man called Ron Gray, who made me feel so welcome.

He looked a big intimidating fellow to my fifteen year old eyes, but he came over with a great big smile on his face and instantly put me at ease. The warm welcome I got from Ron was just what I needed and he lifted my mood even higher, when he took me to stay the night with the rest of the team in a hotel in central London. It was an amazing experience as we travelled through London, seeing the huge buildings and witnessing the pace of life as thousands of people went about their business.

It all seemed very different to what I was used to in Carlisle and whilst it was exciting, it also felt a little daunting and it was reassuring to have Ron close at hand. Not only was London a new experience for me, I had never stayed in a proper hotel before and I was a bit nervous as to the protocol. The only place I had stayed in at this point was a cheap bed and breakfast in Blackpool and although the hotel in London was probably a fairly basic place, it seemed like the Ritz to me.

Fortunately Ron took me under his wing and made sure that I was well looked after. I began to relax and soon had the most amazing meal and after a nice hot bath it was soon time for bed. Though despite the long journey south, I wasn't tired and hardly slept a wink, as I was so excited about the impending game.

When I pulled on my football boots the next day, I felt immediately at ease, I might not have been used to the cosmopolitan life in London and to staying in fancy hotels, but on the football pitch I was definitely in my own environment. I wasn't at all nervous and the standard of football was one which I was more

www.cultfigurepublishing.com

than comfortable in. I played up-front and scored in a 2-1 victory, I was pleased with my performance and felt that as well as my goal, I had also made a good contribution to play and done myself justice.

I returned with the rest of the squad back to Ipswich, which was another new experience as the team travelled on a bus which seemed to me to be more like a limousine. The rest of the lads in the team seemed like a decent bunch and I began to feel really at home. When I arrived back to Ipswich I was taken to meet Mr Robson – the 'Boss.' As with Ron Gray I immediately felt at ease in his company.

He sat me down in his office and made a fuss of me and he had a nice easy manner about him. It felt like I was in the company of a kindly relative rather than someone who was in charge. My previous experience of a 'Boss' was through the dead-end jobs I had been doing and generally consisted of some hard-case who spent all day barking orders at everyone. Mr Robson obviously did things very differently.

He asked me how I thought I had done in the trial, although I really didn't know what to say and so just stood there. Picking up that I was a shy, reserved lad, the 'Boss' got straight to the point. 'I have received a good account of you,' he said. 'I would like you to play football for me' and with that I was handed my first contract as an apprentice professional footballer.

I immediately accepted the offer, I had felt so at home and so welcome and I felt like I was becoming part of a family rather than a football club. The whole weekend had been wonderful and the only thing that I might have changed about the whole experience was catching sight of big Ron wandering around the hotel in his long-johns. It had only been a week after my Liverpool disappointment and it was to be an early introduction to the peaks and troughs of the great game. I had been through a range of emotions and I suppose it all encapsulated what the game was about and was good practice for what was to lie ahead.

I later learned that over in Liverpool the truth was beginning to emerge about why I hadn't arrived. Bill Shankly had thought I couldn't be bothered to come and obviously decided not to pursue his interest. After further investigation it became apparent that a scout at the club hadn't turned up to meet me and Liverpool were keen to get in touch with me and were set to offer me a contract.

The football grapevine was obviously buzzing and Ipswich Town were obviously aware of this. Their scout John Carruthers had obviously tipped off the 'Boss' not only about my play, but also about the fact that Liverpool were interested and he knew that if he didn't move fast, he would lose me. Hence the quick offer of a contract, which I heard later, was much to the annoyance of Bill Shankly.

I arrived back at Ipswich the following week, I was still only fifteen years of age and was a little wary of life in a new town on my own. I obviously didn't know anyone and so I was not only having to cope with new surroundings I was also having to deal with facing the demands of being an apprentice footballer. As well as playing, we had to clean football boots, mop out the dressing rooms and sweep the terraces after a game. One or two of the other lads didn't seem to like doing this and whilst it wasn't at the top of my list of things to do either, I never found it a problem. I had of course been working in similar jobs and so was used to getting my hands dirty and performing menial tasks for a living.

Cyril Lea, was the assistant to the 'Boss' at the time and he always ensured that everyone was on their toes. We always had to be smartly turned out and our work was always inspected so as to see that it was up to scratch. The work was tough, but I was determined to be a success. I had seen how my Mum and Dad lived and I had experienced first hand via the 'chippy' job how hard life could be and I was in no rush to go back for more.

On the pitch I fitted in well and loved everything about being a full time footballer, I found the standard of football to my liking and word soon spread about the hot new prospect and a number of the senior players at the time like David Best and Peter Morris took an interest in how I was doing. During training sessions, they would often ask about the youth team games that I had played in and enquire as to how things had gone.

I remember once following a game against Cambridge United, they asked me what the score had been and I told them that we had won the game 6-0. They asked me if I scored any and I shrugged my shoulders before admitting that I had scored all six. The lads were really pleased, although I didn't know how to react. I wasn't used to people making a fuss of me and in the end I went red with embarrassment.

I was adapting well to the life of an apprentice footballer, although I didn't find adapting to life away from the club so straightforward and I was soon feeling restless. The main reason was the accommodation I was living in which was only a small place. It also seemed to be overflowing with people, as not only was it home to the landlady and her kids, but half a dozen other apprentices also lived there.

The place wasn't to my liking, as there was no privacy and no room to breath. I was the last to move in and so everyone else was established and so I also felt a bit left out. I was missing a few of my mates back in Carlisle and I started to get homesick and so one night I decided that I'd had enough and went home. I couldn't afford the train ticket, so without telling anyone at the club, I started to hitch-hike and eventually arrived back in Carlisle the next day.

Obviously the club soon found out that I had gone AWOL and tracked me down. I might have expected a bollocking, or have the club give up on me. Instead the 'Boss' was concerned and sent John Carruthers over to see me.

I suppose it may have looked like a strange decision to have temporarily turned my back on such a great opportunity in Ipswich. However I have always been someone who has gone with gut instincts, rather than sitting down and looking at a wider context. I wasn't happy and so I decided to go somewhere where I thought I would be better off.

I had a long chat with John and told him of my concerns. In all honesty there wasn't an awful lot going for me back in Carlisle and I was never really going to stay up there. However he assured me that I would get some new digs and how highly regarded I was at the club and with a minimum of fuss from all concerned, I headed back to Suffolk.

When I arrived at my new digs, I was met by a kindly looking lady named Mrs Strawn. She had a warm look in her eyes and a friendly easy-going manner and I immediately felt that this was somewhere I was going to be happy. Her home was spotlessly clean and within two minutes of my arrival, Mrs Strawn told me in a rich cockney accent to call her Vera. I soon had a sandwich in one hand and a cup of tea in the other and I immediately felt at home.

She was absolutely brilliant and I lived there for the next seven years – in fact the only reason I moved out was because I eventually got married. Vera became very much a second Mum to me, there were always clean clothes on my back, good food on the table, a cuddle when I felt down and a telling off when I stepped out of line. I also became best pals with Vera's son Steve, who was the same age as me. Steve had a good sense of humour and provided a nice release from football, as we were two daft lads together. For example, I once bought a tape recorder which rather than play music on, Steve used as a means to record his farts. It was all innocent fun and I believe that the settled home life I had at this time helped me enjoy things at Ipswich and make my early time at the club such a success.

Across the road from where I was living there was a youth club and not long after my arrival Steve decided to take me over and we soon spent all our spare time there. There was plenty to do, although I used to leave early as I was on a curfew from the club, much to the amusement of the other lads who would always give me plenty of grief about this. One evening whilst I was there I met a girl named Maggie. I thought that she was fantastic and it was a case of love at first sight, we found that we got on well and soon began spending a lot of time with each other.

All of a sudden I had a lot going for me, a clean and friendly place to live, a lovely girlfriend and a burgeoning career as an apprentice professional footballer. It's really important to me to feel settled and I honestly don't think I would have stayed in Ipswich if things hadn't gone so well with the move to the Strawn's and also meeting Maggie.

They were not the only ones to help at this time, as I had literally arrived in Ipswich as Sir Bobby Robson was to later say with: 'My arse hanging out of my trousers and a shilling in my pocket.' The only possessions I brought down to Ipswich with me were an old pair of brown football boots that I used to play in, which I believe the 'Boss' threw straight in the bin.

It hadn't bothered me, or even been something that I had noticed before, as everyone around me in Carlisle also lived in poverty and struggled to make ends meet. All of a sudden I was in a different environment, where it was clear that I was a lot worse off financially than many of my colleagues and at times it felt a bit embarrassing. Even as a youth team player I was expected to arrive at games wearing a collar and tie, the only problem was that in the early days I didn't have either.

However the 'Boss' (I still can't bring myself to call him anything else even today when we meet) noticed my predicament and soon sorted me out. He bought me a couple of nice shirts and some lovely silk ties and it helped make me feel part of things and boost my confidence. An Italian hairdresser called Gino often popped over to the club to cut some of the first team players hair. He had a fashionable shop in the town, covered in photographs of his clients and it seemed that anyone who was a name in the area got their hair cut there. Soon I was going there too and the process of feeling part of something, which is also very important to me, was on its way.

The process was completed a couple of months later when I saved up my wages (a fiver a week) and went to the Army and Navy store in Ipswich and bought my first suit. It felt at the time like a monumental amount, albeit only six pounds. The 'Boss' complimented me on how smart I was and I felt the proverbial million dollars. I not only felt good, but I was also beginning to feel like a footballer and that I had come along way from being a 'chippy' from Carlisle who had nothing to his name.

As well as helping me smarten up my image, the 'Boss' was always there for advice and encouragement. I had obviously never played under a professional manager before and the insight into the game he provided helped me no end. We soon developed a great relationship and the 'Boss' christened me 'The Diamond.' He was ecstatic about my progress although my fellow Ipswich youth-team colleagues were not always so complimentary.

It was mainly good natured banter, as I was subjected to wolf whistling and calls of 'Bobby's boy,' although there were a few more serious digs, as one or two of the lads seemed to think I got special treatment. I have to disagree, as I remember that I was always being told by the 'Boss' to keep my feet on the ground.

I was very keen and enthusiastic and like a lot of lads, also impatient and so the 'Boss' had a job on his hands trying to reign me in. I was desperate for that first team place and every week that passed without me getting it, saw my impatience grow. I was never sulky or petulant about it I was just desperate to get on the park and play football to the highest standard that I possibly could.

I do remember that my wages at the time were a fiver a week and that the 'Boss' used to double it, so long as I cleaned his car once a week. I suppose it was his way of looking after me with a few extra pounds, but giving it to me in a way that still kept me grounded. It was because he had looked after me so well that I had always seen the 'Boss' as a very easy-going person. I was therefore somewhat shocked to see another side to his personality when the first team suffered a 4-2 defeat at home to a rampant Leeds United side.

I was on duty with the other members of the youth team and all set to clean out the dressing-rooms and sweep the terraces

after the game had finished. As the final whistle went, I was near
to the tunnel when I heard a commotion, two of the senior Ipswich
Town players, Tommy Carroll and Bill Baxter had become involved
in a confrontation with the 'Boss' and his assistant Cyril Lea.

Things soon escalated from a verbal scenario and a punch
was thrown at the 'Boss.' I was still only just turned sixteen and
so unsure of what I should do, did I help, or did I mind my own
business? I wasn't sure what the protocol was, I certainly felt like
stepping in to get stuck into Carroll and Baxter that's for sure. In
the end it didn't matter, as the 'Boss' and Cyril soon had the better
of things and Baxter and Carroll were soon on their way out of
Ipswich.

The 'Boss' could clearly see that I was shocked by events,
however he told me it was nothing to worry about and all part of
the hurly-burly world of football. As he had been so kind to me
in the past I had always respected him, however if anything I now
respected him even more. It was clear that the 'Boss' was going
to run the club his way and part of that process involved discarding
older players some of whom had created something of a clique and
bringing through youngsters like myself.

I was offered full professional terms and my days of sweeping
the terraces and cleaning boots were over. In fact some of my
former fellow youth-team players were now cleaning my boots,
which was a strange experience for me, but not as strange as for
my old pals. It didn't go down well with some, but I saw it as their
problem, not mine, as all I wanted to do was play football.

I was now earning a basic wage of twenty-five pounds a week
which rose to thirty-five if we won. This was an awful lot of
money to me and I vowed that the days of my 'arse hanging out
of my trousers' as had been the case when I had arrived only a

year earlier were over. I treated myself to a couple of nice suits and set about saving for a car. I was also able to help my parents back home and began sending them some money each week. It felt good that my new situation was not just helping me but also my family, so I became extremely upset when I found out that my Dad was spending the money that I had been sending back on drink and my Mum was going without.

His drinking had got worse and he had started knocking my Mum around. There were a couple of incidents when I had been at home, but I wasn't big enough to do much about it and I turned a blind eye to things. However I had vowed that when I was big enough, I would sort things out. I was by then training full-time at the club and living on a diet of fillet steak and fresh vegetables at the Strawn's. I was in great physical shape, had filled out from a boy to a man and was as strong as a bull. I'm not proud to admit it, but I went home one weekend and sorted my Dad out and made sure he never laid a finger on my Mum again.

On the football front, I had progressed from the youth team to playing for the reserve team where I continued to play up-front. I was banging in the goals, and with better pitches to play on, regular training and a never-ending supply of good food, I was blossoming. Although one thing that soon changed was that my days as a striker were over. This happened during the pre-season before the 1972/3 season, when the 'Boss' told me he would like to play me in the back four in a practice game.

I thought I had been performing well up-front and I couldn't understand what he was thinking about and I had never seen myself as a defender. Whilst I was very dubious and even more confused, I was happy to play where I was told. I have never understood footballers who kick up a stink about where they play and I would have gone in goal if asked and been happy to do so.

Whilst I started in my new role of a defender with a degree of caution, the feeling soon disappeared as I immediately felt at ease. The game was a complete revelation for me, as previously I had been used to playing with my back to the goal and when I received the ball, having to turn some big lumbering centre-half who was trying to kick lumps out of me.

I was now playing facing the goal and could see everything opening up before me. All sorts of possibilities now seemed available, I could still get forward, which I enjoyed doing, as I was comfortable on the ball and once I got a head of steam going I was capable of making runs from my own six-yard box to well inside the opposition half. Most defenders hated this and were not sure what to do.

Alternatively I was equally happy to play a long cross-field ball and open things up that way, or else keep it nice and simple and play it to someone else close by. There were so many options and it was a wonderful feeling. The 'Boss' had been correct and even though I had been playing well up-front, I felt that I was going to make much more of an impact at the back. In fact, I would say that I genuinely felt that this was what I was born to do.

The 'Boss' had actually been forced into looking for an alternative position for me, as he knew that Colin Harper, who was the left-back at the time, would be suspended for the first few games of the new season. It was by now the summer of 1972 and Colin had been sent off towards the end of the previous season. In his frustration he had also thrown his shirt at the referee and was obviously looking at a lengthy ban. There weren't too many naturally left-footed players around and so the 'Boss' had limited options.

Like a lot of young players I was also desperate to make the step up into the first team, so I suppose the 'Boss' didn't have too much to lose by giving me an opportunity. It was still a surprise though when I was invited on an overseas tour with the first team to Spain. It was only a few weeks until the new season started and it proved to be a wonderful experience, as not only was it great to be part of the first team set-up, it was also my first trip abroad.

I was still very unworldly in those days and as I had never flown before was a bit overawed by it all. I actually daren't leave my seat once we were airborne, even though I was bursting for the toilet. The trip was a chance for everyone to let off steam and bond over a few beers. I had never particularly been interested in booze before, but I think that this was the first time that I could see the attraction. I enjoyed having a laugh and a joke with my mates and I enjoyed the feeling you get when you have had a few pints and you begin to relax and lose your inhibitions. It was also great to be amongst friends and having a good time away from home.

It wasn't all fun and games though, as I remember that there were a lot of Cockney lads over there and one evening one of them had a go at me. We were about to get into a bit of a tussle, but I couldn't work out what his problem was, so I came straight out with it and asked him. It turned out that he had heard my accent and thought that I was German, so he obviously wasn't the brightest. When I told him that I was from Carlisle and part of the Ipswich Town end of season tour, he apologised and wanted to be my best pal. All I wanted was a good time with no hassle and so I let it pass.

It wasn't the only incident on the tour though, as one evening our centre-half, Derek 'Chopper' Jefferson, a hard-drinking, wild-man, was sent home after he became involved in some aggravation in a bar with some tourists. The 'Boss' was very strict about players setting an example, especially when they were representing the club.

As a result Derek never played for us again and was later transferred to Wolves. Many years later I heard that Derek had become a born again Christian and was working as a Minister. I always got on well with him although he didn't earn his nickname for nothing and you would have got big odds on his choice of future profession believe you me.

It seemed fate was taking a hand, as with Derek's departure another opening in the back four had now presented itself to me. I had made great progress at the club and I was soon invited to travel with the first-team up to Manchester United for the opening league fixture of the 1972/3 season. I went there thinking that I was there to help the trainer sort the kit out and it was great to be part of things. I was awestruck as we pulled up to the magnificent Old Trafford stadium and I was in a daze when the 'Boss' named the team that was playing that afternoon.

A couple of the lads came up and began congratulating me and I wasn't sure why as I was busy lapping up the atmosphere and hadn't been listening. It turned out that I was playing and I had been selected at left full-back. I was due to mark the Scottish international winger Willie Morgan, who was part of a Manchester United team featuring legends such as Denis Law, Bobby Charlton and George Best.

There was very little said and no time for nerves, the 'Boss' just told me to get out there and do my thing, although he did boost my confidence by telling me that I had too much pace and power for Morgan to trouble me. I was thrilled and just wanted to get on with it as this was the moment I had been waiting for. To get the opportunity to make my debut at Old Trafford also made it seem extra special.

The only concern I had, was that I wanted my Mum and Dad to be there to witness my big day. Despite the recent problems, I still wanted them to share my special moment, however the 'Boss' in typical fashion had arranged everything and he told me that my parents were already safely seated in the ground and were waiting to see me strut my stuff. A number of players during the Robson era made their debut at Old Trafford – no doubt a shrewd piece of psychology from the 'Boss,' as if you can handle the pressure there, you can no doubt handle it anywhere.

I remember emerging from the tunnel to be hit by a wall of sound and a mass of red and white, as the huge crowd roared encouragement to their United heroes. It proved to be a dream debut for me, as I made the opening goal after only eight minutes. I intercepted a pass intended for Willie Morgan and went marauding forward, in the style which had the 'Boss' soon giving me another nickname, namely that of 'The Six O'Clock Express.'

I delivered an inch perfect forty-yard cross field ball for Trevor Whymark, who brought the ball down and coolly slotted it away to silence the home supporters. We deserved to be in front and totally dominated the game and with six minutes of the game left Bryan Hamilton clinched it for us when he added a second. By the time Denis Law scored a consolation goal four minutes later, half of the ground was empty, as the United fans had started to file their way out of the stadium and had begun making their way home.

Although United were a team on the wane at this point, it was still a great victory and a dream come true for me. It hadn't been long since I had played on park pitches in Carlisle, so to be on the same park as a team of their stature was a phenomenal experience. Although I have to say it wasn't an overwhelming one as I enjoyed every minute of it and was hungry for more.

Whilst I wasn't overawed, I was still appreciative of great football players and after the game I was delighted to be in the company of some football legends and I wandered around the player's lounge collecting autographs. One of the first players I made a bee-line for was Bobby Charlton, who had always been a hero of mine. It hadn't seemed long ago that as a schoolboy I had watched Bobby play his part in the magnificent 1966 World Cup win and here I was having played against him.

He delighted me by not only giving me his autograph, but also telling me how impressed he was with my performance, before adding that I would be the one signing autographs in the future. On the way home it was customary for the players to have a few beers on the team bus, the 'Boss' told me I could have a couple, but with the adrenalin flowing and the lads spurring me on, I practically fell off the bus when we arrived back at Portman Road. It was a wonderful day and one I will never forget.

I was soon made painfully aware of the nature of football in my second appearance several days later, when we were beaten 2-1 at home to our bitter rivals Norwich City. It was bad enough to be beaten, but I also gave away a penalty, which proved to be decisive as it turned out to be the winning goal. I was of course devastated, but the rest of the lads were fantastic about it, as was the 'Boss.' No one blamed or criticised me and it was just accepted that it was one of those things that occurs.

The 'Boss' told me to learn from it and to make sure it never happened again. I listened to his words and it remained the only penalty I was to give away during my entire career. I managed to overcome this brief setback and continued being selected for the first team and by the end of the month I had notched my first ever league goal in a thrilling 3-3 draw away at Leeds United. Elland Road was notorious for providing an incredibly intimidating atmosphere as the Leeds fans roared their heroes on. However if you had shut your eyes when I scored, you would have thought you were in the local library, as you couldn't hear a thing.

The goal came following a corner, which had managed to loop beyond the far post. I couldn't believe my luck as it arrived at my feet and there was no mistake as I buried it first time. I ran to the small band of Ipswich fans that had made the journey and punched the air in delight. It was extra special as I smashed it home with my right foot which was supposedly my weaker side.

I put in a great performance and following the game, I overheard the then Leeds United manager Don Revie having a conversation with the 'Boss.' 'Bloody hell Bobby' he said, 'Where have you got him from?' Before asking half seriously, 'How much do you want for him?' The 'Boss' replied by telling Mr Revie that he didn't have enough money to buy me. It was a nice compliment and one which I appreciated.

I was enjoying every single minute of being a professional footballer and every week saw me lining up against players I had previously only seen on television. It had not seemed like many years ago that I had imagined I was Peter Osgood and Peter Bonetti as I charged around the playing-fields in Botcherby. Now here I was playing against them in the top-flight. Fantasy had actually become reality, as I played against them three times during my first season. Unfortunately we lost to them twice, once in the league and once in the fourth round of the FA Cup. However I did manage to score against them in a 3-0 home victory at Portman Road.

It was equally surreal, albeit for different reasons when we played a game against Coventry City and were losing at home 1-0. We were under the cosh and not playing at all well when suddenly the floodlights went off and the match had to be abandoned. People said that the club had deliberately had the lights doctored, which is of course ridiculous. It did not stop it becoming a controversial incident, which for Coventry was made worse, when a week later we comfortably won a rearranged fixture 2-0.

Things were going well for me, so much so, that the 'Boss' was soon comparing me to the likes of Bobby Moore and Duncan Edwards – both giants of the game. Sentiments which were echoed by other respected football names of the time. With the most notable individual who had noticed me undoubtedly being Sir Alf Ramsey. I had made only a dozen or so appearances for Ipswich Town when he selected me for the England under-23 team.

I was only concerned about cementing my place at club level at this point, so to obtain international recognition was totally unexpected. The under-23 team played a very big part in the international set-up in those days. It was a very different time to now, where young lads of seventeen and eighteen can find themselves in the full international team. Back then younger players were blooded against lads of similar age and experience and it was seen as a tremendous honour for me to have been selected as I had so little first team experience under my belt.

In those days you were informed by a letter which was sent to the club, so the mail that morning brought a lovely surprise. I did think that it was a wind-up at first, but after checking with officials at the club, it was found to be authentic and I travelled over to

Wales to meet up with the rest of the squad. It was brilliant to be pulling on the famous white jersey and we eventually beat a Welsh side 3-0, in a comfortable victory at Swansea.

It was another jump up in standard, but again it seemed very natural for me. Other people seemed to expect me to be fazed by things, but I have to say that it never bothered me and I felt comfortable with it all. I have never particularly thought about why that was so, although maybe when you have come from humble beginnings as I have, where even food on the table is not a given, then it helps give you a perspective on things. When you have worried about fundamental things like whether you might be eating that evening, everything else seems rather straightforward after that.

It seemed that I could do no wrong and that every game I played in, I did something to make the football community sit up and take notice. I was delivering confident assured performances in the back four and showing maturity beyond my tender years. Many of the central-defenders of the time, were the strong rugged types and as the cliché goes, were not particularly able to play football, but could stop those that could.

Ball playing central-defenders that were able to get forward and were comfortable on the ball were a rarity and my style of play was certainly getting me noticed. I was shackling many of the top strikers of the day as part of my defensive duties and also carving out a reputation for instigating insightful attacking play. So much so, that whenever I began tearing forward, a roar of anticipation would erupt from the crowd, as they knew that something was likely to happen.

I also chipped in with a few goals and remember scoring a beauty versus Derby County, which encapsulated all which was good about my style of play. I won the ball in my own half and then broke free and began tearing towards the Derby goal. I played a one/two with one of the lads, although the return pass I received was not the best. However in a fifty/fifty tackle, I brushed aside Colin Todd – a tremendous player himself and powered forward before smashing an unstoppable thirty-yard shot which breezed past the 'keeper and into the net where it stuck in the stanchion. Even the Derby fans applauded.

The rest of the lads mobbed me and for a moment I realised how good it must be to play as a professional striker. That adrenaline rush you get and the reaction in others you provoke after a goal is like no other. As a defender you can have people appreciate what you do, but when was the last time you saw someone get mobbed by their team-mates, or have the crowd erupt in raptures as a result of a good tackle?

It was a fantastic first season, which ended with us finishing fourth in the league, twelve points behind the champions Liverpool. This was the club's highest top-flight finish since 1961/2 when the club had won the league under Sir Alf Ramsey. It also saw us bring some silverware back to Portman Road as we clinched the Texaco Trophy (later renamed the Anglo Scottish Cup) after a 4-2 aggregate win.

It was a competition held for teams that had not qualified for Europe the previous season and whilst it was not as prestigious as some trophies, it was nice to be a winner. Especially as our opponents in the two-legged final were our great rivals Norwich City. We were actually presented with the trophy straight after the second game which was held at Carrow Road. The stadium was practically empty as the Norwich fans had all left. However, it didn't prevent our band of travelling supporters enjoying themselves. I actually think they got more of a buzz from seeing us turn over our old enemies on their patch than if we had won at Portman Road.

We would not get to defend our crown, but for all the right reasons, as our league position ensured that we qualified for the UEFA Cup for the first time in the club's history. I had enjoyed a terrific season personally and was a virtual ever present making 48 full and 1 substitute appearance and to cap a wonderful season I was named the club's player of the season.

I was also picked to represent England in what was termed 'The Little World Cup,' which was held in Barcelona, where I got to line up alongside the likes of Trevor Francis and my old mate from Liverpool, Phil Thompson. It was essentially a World Cup style tournament for players under-21 years of age. It was a lovely experience topped off when we beat West Germany 2-1 in the final.

I don't know what you get for winning a World Cup these days, but we received a wrist watch each, an illustration of how times have changed. Although I suppose I do have the honour of being able to lay claim to being a World Cup winner of sorts, even if I didn't get my hands on the big one.

Upon my return to England, I received a reminder as to how lucky I was, when a lad called Kenny Sharp came to see me. We had played together in the youth team at Ipswich Town and for a time he had shared digs with me at the Strawn's house. However, on this occasion, it was not a social visit as Kenny had come to say goodbye, as he had been released by the club. I always thought that Kenny was a decent player and was sure he was good enough to make the grade. I felt really sorry for him and the incident really brought home to me how fragile a footballer's life is and I was determined to get my head down and keep it all going.

One thing that I managed to keep fairly quiet at this time was the fact that my eyesight was really poor. Away from the pitch, I needed to wear glasses, which was obviously not something that I could do whilst I played. I tried wearing contact lenses during games, but in those days they were very primitive and I found them uncomfortable to wear. They also kept popping out, especially when I headed the ball, so in the end I stopped using them.

Obviously laser surgery wasn't an option in those days, so I had no alternative but to play with less than perfect vision. Things were fine close up, but play at a distance was very blurred, for example I often saw 'double' and as a defender, I sometimes saw what appeared to be two players running with the ball at me. Fortunately I always tackled the 'right' one and it was never something that became an issue. Obviously people are amazed when I tell them today that I went through my career playing this way. However I got on with it and just accepted there wasn't too much I could do about it.

In a funny way, I actually think it made me a better player, as it improved my awareness and intuition and I developed a sixth sense about where I should be. I certainly didn't want it to become public knowledge though, as it could have given opposition players an advantage, so I kept it quiet and continued with the job in hand, namely playing football.

I also tried to keep my habit of smoking a packet of cigarettes a day secret, but one day was rumbled by the 'Boss' who caught me having a crafty smoke. I told him that I was merely holding it for my central defensive partner Allan Hunter who also smoked like a chimney. The 'Boss' wasn't buying that and he wasn't very happy, but as I had been made the player of the year, it wasn't something that could be said to be hampering my performance.

Although he did add that if my form began to dip then he would blame the cigarettes and they would have to go. Fortunately, like my poor eyesight, it never became an issue, which is just as well, as I don't think I could have given them up, especially as at the time most of my cigarettes arrived free gratis.

There was a large cigarette factory called Churchman's, which at the time was situated beside Portman Road and as I arrived for training, the girls who worked there would throw down packets of cigarettes from the windows, which me and Allan Hunter used to go and smoke in the hut that the groundsman used, before we started our training.

I liked to arrive at training early and before I got down to it, I always enjoyed having a nice pot of tea and a few cigarettes. I would read the morning newspapers and have a chat with one or two of the other smokers and generally ease myself into the day. I'm not sure it would be the recommended way for footballers to start things now however it didn't do me any harm. I always needed a nicotine fix and it was the only way that I could get myself started in the morning. I was only nineteen at the time but had incredibly already been smoking for eight years.

It was around this time that the club also began looking at things like training and diet. I had up until this point always enjoyed eating a fillet steak for my pre-match meal, as had a few of the other players. However the 'Boss' discovered that they took up to eight hours to digest and so he was keen to put a stop to it all.

It didn't go down well with me, as at the time I practically lived on fillet steak and I always got Mrs Strawn at the digs to knock me one up. My food and lodging was paid for by the club and the 'Boss' made sure that I always had plenty of nice food to eat, much to the annoyance of her son Steve, whose food obviously wasn't paid for. As a result, I would often be tucking into my steak meal with all the trimmings, whilst Steve would be presented with a plate of something less glamorous.

I was always mindful of how it had been back home in Carlisle when a meal could be a rarity and so when there was good food on the table I was always first in the queue. The steak dinners wouldn't work for everyone, but they were certainly doing me no harm and in my opinion it really is a case of each to their own. For example, I remember once speaking to Ted Phillips, the great Ipswich Town striker from the 1960s and he told me his pre-match meal often consisted of: Sausage, eggs, beans and chips.

A few of the players began experimenting and they ate different types of food before games, for example Mick Mills would eat a bowl of rice pudding. It might have done the trick for him, but it was no good to me and so I went in to see the 'Boss.' Mindful of the fact that I had just been voted player of the year I think he was happy to let me have what ever I wanted, so long as I continued to do the business.

He didn't want the rest of the lads seeing me still on the steak though and so at home fixtures I used to collect my food from a local butcher on a Friday evening and eat it at home. During away fixtures I was forced to eat my pre-match meal out of the way where the rest of the lads couldn't see me.

My second full season at Town in 1973/4 was soon underway and I was raring to go. We kicked off proceedings with a pre-season trip to Guernsey and then a tour of Norway. It was a feature of my time at the club, that we always had plenty of tours abroad. The 'Boss' enjoyed his trips away and he knew that they were effective in terms of bonding, they were also a money-spinner for the club. It was always something that I was personally appreciative of as I had barely been out of Carlisle until my arrival at the club.

A month later, we got the opportunity to travel overseas again, when we kicked off our UEFA Cup campaign. The first round draw pitted us against the mighty Real Madrid and everyone at the club was obviously excited at the prospect. It was fantastic to be playing in such illustrious company and even better as we beat them 1-0 in the first leg at Portman Road, following a Trevor Whymark goal. Trevor was an excellent striker and can count himself very unlucky not to have added to his solitary England cap.

In the away leg at the Bernabeu Stadium we were treated to a tour of the ground. It was a magnificent arena and the club trophy cabinet seemed to be bigger than the dressing rooms at Portman Road. On the evening of the game, we played in front of a capacity crowd of 80,000 people, who generated a fantastic atmosphere. The 'Boss' warned us that we would be under a lot of pressure as Real needed to win the game and told us to keep calm and to keep our shape.

I was someone who liked to get forward, however the 'Boss' told me that I would have to curtail my natural instincts. We were under the cosh for large parts of the game, but a superb defensive performance, in which I feel I played my part, ensured we held out for a 0-0 draw. As we had won the first leg, we were through to the next round on aggregate.

In the next round we faced Lazio and in the first game at Portman Road we thumped them 4-0, with Trevor Whymark scoring all four goals. They were baying for blood in the return leg at the Olympic Stadium in Rome and employed all the usual tactics to try and disrupt our preparation following our arrival. We had been put in a hotel near to a main ring-road and their fans spent the evening before the game shouting and screaming whilst driving around in cars blaring out music and sounding off horns.

On the night of the game itself, the atmosphere was extremely intimidating and as we emerged from the tunnel, the Italian supporters went crazy. I remember wanting to get on the pitch as soon as possible as a torrent of spit and missiles came our way.

Before the game started there was to be a presentation, although I wasn't sure what for. However it turned out that the President of Roma, who share the same stadium and are of course Lazio's bitter rivals was to present a trophy to Trevor Whymark in honour of his four goals in the first leg. Apparently the trophy was inscribed with the message 'With friendship and gratitude from the supporters of AS Roma.'

If the Lazio fans were going crazy before they now went completely berserk. I know my eyesight wasn't the best, but I swear that I saw someone waving a gun in the crowd and I seriously thought we were going to be lucky to get home in one piece. The game itself was later dubbed 'The Battle of Rome' and it seemed that the Lazio players were as crazy as their supporters. Challenges were flying in, which was fine by me, however it was all the other shenanigans which got me going, such as spitting, shirt pulling and diving in order to get a free-kick or penalty. To be honest, football went by the wayside and the game got out of control. I remember one of their players, Giorgio Chinaglia who was of Italian descent, but had actually been born in Wales, particularly putting himself about. Chinaglia was born in Swansea and had played for them against us in the league the season before.

He had seemed a nice fellow then, but with a Lazio shirt on his back he had turned into a demon, although he wasn't the worst by any means.

It seemed like Cyril Lea, our trainer, was on and off the pitch attending to someone every two minutes. By far the worst injury was sustained by our striker David Johnson, when a Lazio player stamped on a particularly tender part of his body and he obtained a wound that required eight stitches. I was to later joke that I didn't think 'Johnno,' was big enough down there to accommodate one stitch, let alone eight.

Joking aside, the 'Boss' was furious at the Lazio players antics. A couple of them even tried to have a go after the match and as a result he put in an official complaint to FIFA. I suppose what really mattered was that although we eventually lost the game 4-2 we had done enough at Portman Road to secure our passage through to the next round.

After the game we were advised to hang around for a couple of hours and let the Lazio fans disperse. We were also advised to stay out of the way and not go anywhere close to the city centre, so we headed out of town into the suburbs. I felt we'd earned a couple of beers and whilst I wasn't looking for trouble, I wasn't going to be locked away in a hotel room either. I was having a pint with Allan Hunter and a couple of other lads, when in marched a gang of Lazio supporters.

I thought that we were on for some trouble and got ready just in case. Fortunately they were a decent set of lads and had only come over to congratulate us on our performance and tell us that we were an excellent side. I was later to hear that there were riots all over town and a coach carrying Ipswich Town supporters was pelted with stones so we were very lucky.

I genuinely thought we were going to win the trophy that season, as we soon despatched Dutch side, FC Twente 3-1 on aggregate in the next round. They were a lovely team, who contained a certain Arnold Muhren in their ranks and although not the most fashionable name in the competition, were still an excellent scalp for us to take. Obviously the 'Boss' was impressed, as Arnold was to eventually make his way to Portman Road, where with Frans Thijssen he enjoyed a phenomenal career.

In the quarter-final game we were drawn against Locomotiv Leipzig of East Germany. They were a strong athletic team and hard to break down, but in a tight game at Portman Road, I scored the only goal as we beat them 1-0. The return leg was an eye-opener, as it meant a trip behind what was known then as the 'Iron Curtain.' The poverty was incredible and I felt for the locals, as I knew from my own experiences how hard it was when money was tight. We even had to take over our own food, as even basic things like a loaf of bread or a joint of meat were not always in full supply.

It was a freezing cold evening when we played and players were wearing tights and gloves. That wasn't my style and as always, I played in a short-sleeved shirt. There was nothing deliberate about it, but it definitely sent out a message that I meant business. I was the only player on the park to wear a short-sleeved shirt and I think it intimidated a lot of the German players who obviously didn't know what to make of me.

It was again a very tight affair and the poor weather conditions made it even more difficult to play attractive flowing football. However the advantage switched to them when we were reduced to only ten men after Mick Mills was sent off after only 40 minutes. They were a very physical side and we were up against it to contain them and in many ways did well to only lose the game 1-0.

With the aggregate score at one goal each, the match eventually went to penalties. Despite still being a relatively inexperienced player, I was happy to step up and take one and I put mine away with no problems. Unfortunately my central defensive partner Allan Hunter missed his and we were out, it was especially cruel as the big man had been a colossus all evening. Before we left for home, we gave the hotel workers a few quid, as well as the remainder of the food we had taken over with us. You would have thought they had all won the national lottery as we handed things over.

As well as our European adventure, we also had a good run in the FA Cup. We knocked out Sheffield United in the third round with yours truly netting a brace. We were fast approaching half-time and were 1-0 behind, when in quick succession I scored two goals, both headers and both from corners. The goals obviously gave the game a totally different complexion, as we went in leading 2-1, eventually defeating the Blades 3-2. Set-pieces were something that we constantly worked on in training and it was nice to get some reward for all our endeavours on the training ground.

I again scored the winner in the fourth round as we beat Manchester United at Old Trafford. It was the featured game on 'Match of the Day,' so would have been seen by a big audience in an era when football didn't get the televised coverage it does today. So for an evening at least, most people would have been tuned in and watching me in action, which was nice. Following our win at Old Trafford, I thought we might have a chance of winning the trophy, but unfortunately we were to bow out in the fifth round following a lacklustre performance away at Liverpool by a 2-0 margin.

We again finished fourth in the league – this time trailing the eventual winners Leeds United by fifteen points. With a bit more consistency I feel we could have pushed them closer. An example of our erratic form was best illustrated by a terrible 5-0 defeat we suffered away to Leicester City. It was an awful performance and the 'Boss' reacted accordingly.

It had the desired effect and in stark contrast, in our next league game we went to the other extreme and thrashed Southampton 7-0 to equal our club record league victory. It was a perfect game as all eleven players turned in superb performances, which meant that Southampton had no chance and I honestly think that we would have beaten anyone put before us that day.

Despite not enjoying any real success in terms of winning silverware, we did however qualify for the UEFA Cup, so all in all it was a decent enough season for the club. On a personal note, it was to be another fantastic season for me. My form throughout the season had been outstanding and in total I played fifty seven times for the club. I could never understand players who complained about the amount of games they played in, as far as I was concerned I would have played every day if I could.

I was now an established member of the team and had cemented a terrific partnership with the Northern Ireland centre-half Allan Hunter. The 'Boss' christened us 'Bacon and Eggs' and we seemed to have developed a telepathic understanding. On our day I would have backed us against any combination of strikers that you'd care to mention and I think between us we possessed everything you could wish for in a central defensive partnership.

A GREAT START

The Portman Road faithful also appreciated my endeavours and I had become something of a crowd favourite. I scooped my second Ipswich Town player of the year award, which was the first time in the history of the club that anyone had achieved this feat in back to back seasons. It seemed that my good form had also been noticed by the powers that be and I was asked by the 'Boss' to accompany him and other representatives from the club to a function in London, which I assumed was my reward for a good season.

I was told to get hold of a dinner suit and bow-tie, as the function was to be held at the prestigious Hilton hotel in London. Upon our arrival, we were seated in a large ball-room, which was a very luxurious affair and it was only then, that I was told by the 'Boss' that I had been nominated for an award. I did wonder why the name tag on the table containing my moniker had a cross next to it. However it soon became clear, when I was called up onto the stage by Don Revie who told me that I had won and presented me with the award in question.

I had been voted the inaugural PFA Young Footballer of the year, which was a fantastic accolade to have bestowed upon me and is one which has subsequently been awarded to some truly magnificent footballers. With the likes of: Paul Gascoigne, Ryan Giggs, Michael Owen and Wayne Rooney also winning the award.

I was gob-smacked, not only at the nature of such a terrific prize, but also because I didn't know anything about it and so it was totally unexpected. Whilst on stage, Mr Revie again told me how much he rated me as a player and that he thought I would have a long and illustrious career at international level.

I was asked to make a speech, which wasn't something I had done before, but I seemed to say all the right things. When I returned to my seat, I was also told that I had made the PFA select eleven, which is the best team of the season as voted for by my fellow professionals. It meant that I was rated by the opposition and not just my team-mates, which obviously meant a lot to me. I was to be subsequently awarded this honour every season for the next three years.

It was a terrific evening and when I arrived back in Ipswich the next day, the newspapers were full of reports about me and my achievements. All of which suggested that I was going to be around at the top of the game for many years to come. A couple of days later I also won the Rothman's Young Footballer of the year award, so all in all it was a fantastic season for me.

Things off the park were also going well, Maggie and myself had now been courting for several years and we decided to get married, with my mate Steve Strawn acting as the best man. Maggie and I had hit it off from day one and her family had also made me feel welcome. I was now firmly at home in Suffolk and Maggie was a good influence on me. I know a lot of other lads my age were out partying and the like and a few lads back home in Carlisle had gone off the rails, so at this time anyway, I was on the straight and narrow. It seemed I could do nothing wrong and everything was going wonderfully.

If I thought that things couldn't get any better, then I was wrong. I had continued to make excellent progress in the under-23 team and I was requested by Sir Alf Ramsey to attend training with the full England squad. It was less than three years since I had been a 'chippy' in Carlisle so my progress had been phenomenal.

Sir Alf was a gentleman and despite rumours that he could be aloof, I found him to be a very down to earth man. He insisted I call him Alf rather than 'Boss', although I couldn't bring myself to do so, no matter how many times he asked me. He wasn't given to ranting and raving and spoke in a very straight and deliberate manner. It was in the latter days of his time as England manager and he was under pressure to qualify for the World Cup which was to be held in Germany. Although you wouldn't have known this, as at all times he remained calm and assured.

I enjoyed being around seasoned professionals many of whom had been boyhood heroes of mine, although it was one which I took in my stride. Sir Alf was very encouraging, he told me that he been watching me for some time and was very impressed with my abilities as a player and that he thought I would be in the England set-up for many years to come. It would have been lovely to have played for him, but by the time I actually got the call up to the full side, Sir Alf had unfortunately been fired.

Things were rounded off with an end of season club trip to Bermuda, which was my very first long-haul trip abroad. We stayed in a beautiful hotel, by a wonderful golf course. I spent my days, snorkelling, sea-fishing or playing golf and my evenings lounging around drinking expensive cocktails. Life it seemed could get no better. A national newspaper wrote an article on me with the headline 'Kevin Beattie: a man with the world at his feet.' It certainly felt that way, life was sweet and it seemed that I could do no wrong.

As we entered the next season, I felt positive that we could win some silverware and I could build on my growing reputation in the game. It seemed everyone was saying great things about

me and as well as the football writers other publications began
to take an interest. On the 15th August 1974, long before the
phrase entered into public consciousness, Maggie and I were
featured in the Radio Times in an article about, 'Footballers and
their Wives.'

Nowadays they interview the football players from their
country mansion and it all looks very glamorous and over the
top. Then it was a little different, as although I was doing well, I
was still living in a modest club-owned house with Maggie. It did
provide the 'Boss' with the opportunity to again speak in glowing
terms about me. He reiterated his claim that I was the next Bobby
Moore, before cheekily adding 'And just wait until he grows up.'

Despite all the good things that were clearly happening to me,
I never really took much notice of it all. I turned up, pulled on
my boots and did my thing. It all seemed very natural to me. I
think that is what impressed other people, especially the 'Boss,'
who couldn't quite work out how easy it all seemed to come to
me. He had thrown me into the first team, where a lot of young
players find the situation too daunting to cope with, however not
only had I coped, but I had flourished.

I never gave too much thought to it all and just loved what
I was doing, I had been given a great opportunity and I wanted
to make the most of it all and the best of what I had been given.
I had always had a good physique and had plenty of pace and as
a former striker was both comfortable on the ball and happy to
get forward. In training, I was never much of a long distance
runner, although I loved the weights room and also enjoyed
devising my own little routines to help improve my game.

For example, as I was naturally left-footed, I would constantly
kick the ball against a wall with my right-foot so as to improve

that part of my game.

I am only 5ft 10 inches tall but thanks to my training efforts, I soon acquired a reputation as one of the best headers of a ball in the game. I spent hours practising my jumps and soon found the art was all in the timing. I would tie some string around a ball and then balance it so that it sat on the top of a crossbar and see if I could head it. I would jump for hours on end and eventually I got to the point where I could reach the ball.

It never felt like a chore to be doing this kind of thing, I just saw it as a necessary way of improving my game. My efforts were ultimately rewarded and I was eventually able to beat players in the air who were several inches, taller than me. The 'Boss' used to say that I could be playing at Portman Road and I could leap so high, that I would rise over the stand and be able to tell you the time on the town hall clock. A bit of an exaggeration, but a number of other people, the 'Boss' included, have said that they have actually seen me jump so high for a ball that I was actually higher than the crossbar.

Whilst the 'Boss' was always lavish in his praise for me, the rest of the lads were less impressed and were keen to engage in some banter, especially where 'Bobby's blue-eyed boy' was concerned. For example a few of the lads used to jokingly ask if the 'Boss' was in fact my Dad, as he was always saying good things about me.

One day after training, the 'Boss' was again waxing lyrical about me and my prowess in the air, when one of the lads butted in and stopped him as he was in mid-flow. 'Beat might be good in the air' he said, as the 'Boss' looked on, 'However then again, so was Douglas Bader and look what happened to him.' For once, I have to say that even the 'Boss' was lost for words.

I had to laugh and certainly could give as good as I got and the banter never bothered me. However my confidence did take a knock a month into the season during a game against Stoke City. We had won the game 3-1, however it was a controversial affair as Stoke claimed that one of our goals was offside. I also became embroiled in controversy of my own when I broke Stoke striker John Ritchie's leg following a challenge for a loose-ball.

It was an accidental challenge, although I was accused by some in the Stoke camp of deliberately trying to injure him. John subsequently stayed overnight in Ipswich hospital and I was also accused of not being bothered, as I hadn't gone to see him. I was naturally upset and I was not the type of player who deliberately set out to hurt someone, this is borne out by the fact that I was never sent-off during my career and was only booked a handful of times.

As a human being, I genuinely felt for the man and also felt horrified that some quarters were suggesting that I would do something like that on purpose. If I had also known that John had stayed in hospital in Ipswich I would have been to see him. The 'Boss' could see that I was shaken by events and was very supportive. He spoke with me privately and also made public statements through the press defending me from the accusations.

What made it worse was the fact that the challenge ultimately signalled the end of John Ritchie's career. I felt terrible, even though there had been no bad intentions on my behalf and it was on my mind for a while and for the first time in my career, I went onto the pitch without my usual sense of abandon.

I think that most people accepted my explanation of events, although Stoke's then manager Tony Waddington had plenty to say for himself. I could understand that he was upset at losing a player in this way, but I couldn't understand all the flack that I was receiving.

Most people in the football world accepted my explanation of things, however over in Stoke I was public enemy number one. Their fans hadn't forgotten and on our next visit there the atmosphere was very tense and intimidating. The game was a very niggling affair and it was made even worse when Allan Hunter broke Denis Smith's leg – again in an accidental challenge. Both Allan and Denis were extremely tough competitors and it was just one of those unfortunate things that occasionally happen and nobody likes to see occurring.

The Stoke fans saw it differently and were going crazy and as the final whistle went we had to get off the pitch fairly quickly. I thought we were safe, but after the game, as we were heading towards the team bus, a small group of Stoke fans approached us. It is fair to say that they weren't looking for our autographs. I was stood with Allan Hunter and my Dad who had been at the game, when the ringleader came up shouting his mouth off about what he was and wasn't going to do. Unbelievably, he had a young girl, who I presume was his daughter with him.

Big Allan wasn't a fellow to stand for any nonsense, or be intimidated and he told him in no uncertain terms that if the young girl wasn't there he would sort him out and with that the mouth-piece disappeared. A few minutes later he came back with his mates but this time minus the girl. I knew straight away it was going to kick off, for as well as Allan, who was a tough-guy, my old man was no shrinking violet either.

I'm also happy to stand my ground and so within seconds it had erupted. The Stoke fans have a fearsome reputation, however on this occasion this group had met their match. Although I am happy to admit, that I was personally happy, when the dust had settled and we were safely back on the team bus en-route for Ipswich.

The press didn't find out about the trouble with the Stoke fans, however the nature of the game and the subsequent injury to Denis Smith had brought back stories of the earlier incident with John Ritchie. I was encouraged by the 'Boss' to get on with things and whilst my thoughts were with John, I knew that I had done nothing intentional and so I tried to forget about the whole unfortunate incident.

Something that definitely helped improve my mood was when I was made captain for the day when we visited my hometown club Carlisle. It was their one and only season in the top flight and it was great to be going home to play them, as I obviously have great affection for the club. I was especially proud to be wearing the captain's armband, as all my family and friends were watching.

I wasn't sure what reception I would get from the home fans, but I was delighted to receive a fantastic welcome. My sister Norma also gave my team-mate Trevor Whymark a warm welcome, when she came to meet me on the team-bus and took something of a shine to him. Unfortunately for her, Trevor was more interested in the forthcoming game, which didn't deter Norma and for a time we struggled to get her off the bus.

Unfortunately the Carlisle team proved to be as persistent and the result went against us, as they won the game 2-1. Towards the end of the game, I just missed out on claiming an equaliser when I flashed a header inches past the post. After the game I stayed over in Carlisle and headed out for a pint with my Dad and his mates. Someone in the pub asked me if I had missed the late chance on purpose, as I am a Carlisle lad born and bred. As the saying goes, you ask a silly question, you get a silly answer – so I replied 'Yes' and thought no more about it.

However the word was soon out and I was inundated with free drinks all evening from Carlisle fans who were delighted that a local lad was doing what they foolishly believed was his bit to help them remain in the league. I decided to let them believe what they wanted to, although I was of course secretly gutted that we had lost the game. Despite this, it was nice to be back at home and if a few people were getting the beers in because they thought that I'd missed a chance on purpose, then all well and good.

We were soon to embark on another great FA Cup run and we despatched, two of the games then big guns Liverpool and Leeds United en route to a semi-final appearance against West Ham. The Leeds game was an epic affair which took three games to settle, before we eventually won the game 3-2. The third game was played at a neutral venue – Leicester City's Filbert Street, although I missed the game through injury, but of course attended. It was held on an evening when the weather was truly awful and the traffic home was just as bad. To relieve the boredom, I remember that as we were stuck in traffic, I got off the team-bus and started walking down the motorway. People thought that I had taken leave of my senses. However there was a reason, as obviously much of the traffic had come from the game and was heading back to Ipswich, so I took the opportunity to chat to a few supporters, which was always something I enjoyed doing.

The semi-final pitched us against West Ham and was held at Villa Park, it was a tense, scrappy affair and ended up a 0-0 draw, I was terribly disappointed, as I felt we'd had enough possession to win the game. However we ultimately couldn't create anything clear cut to help us get the necessary goal to take us through.

In the replay – held at Stamford Bridge, we were to suffer heartbreak as we were eventually beaten 2-1. Although the final score, doesn't offer a true reflection of the game itself as Bryan Hamilton was denied what was in my opinion a perfectly good goal when he was flagged offside. I also thought that one of their goals should have been disallowed for hand-ball.

I was lucky to stay on the park when in my frustration I swore at referee Clive Thomas. He was a controversial figure and in my opinion one of those referees who liked to be the centre of attention, as far as I was concerned he thought that people had paid money to see him, rather than the players. He subsequently stated that he thought he got it wrong in the semi-final, which is fine. However it made no difference to us and we were out.

I don't think we played particularly well over the two games and if we'd played to the best of our abilities I am certain we would have beaten the Hammers. I was also annoyed that two questionable decisions from Thomas had also played their part. I thought that we were a better side than West Ham and also Fulham who reached the final that year and so the cup was there for the taking. This was borne out when on the final league game of the season we strolled to an easy 4-1 victory when the opponents were none other than West Ham.

To lose an opportunity of reaching a showpiece game such as the FA Cup final was of course a disappointment, especially under such controversial circumstances, although 1975 was the year that disappointment and controversy were something I became used to. This came when a rash decision on my behalf ensured that I made both the front and back pages of the newspapers.

I had been selected to play in an England under-23 game

against Scotland and I was sent a train ticket and told to travel up on my own from Ipswich. This was fairly normal in those days as players were obviously coming from different parts of the country and was something of a money saving exercise as it saved on hotel bills and the like.

It is a sign of how times have changed, as the thought of a player representing his country on international duty and travelling up on his own is obviously now a far-fetched concept. I am sure that we would have all flown up to Scotland together if the fixture was held now.

I was set to report to Pittodrie in Aberdeen for an evening fixture, however I suddenly had a brainstorm and decided to call home to Carlisle for a while. Maggie had recently given birth to our eldest daughter Emma and I hadn't been myself. Emma was the type of baby who cried a lot and I wasn't getting a lot of sleep and as a result I was feeling a bit uptight. I am sure if I had been travelling up with a few of the other players there would have been plenty of banter and I wouldn't have been allowed to dwell on my situation. However I had endured a long journey and had plenty of time on my hands to think things over.

I still had a long way to go to reach Aberdeen from Carlisle and I thought a brief trip home for a few hours might chill me out, so I headed across town to see my Mum and it was good to catch up with her. I also decided to go and see my Dad, who was in the pub. I had only intended to stay an hour or so and to only have a few soft drinks, however I was soon into the swing of things and was clutching a pint of lager in my hand and as is often the case, had soon drunk three or four pints.

As each glass was raised to my lips, there was less and less chance of me making the journey onto Pittodrie. The trip had actually coincided with my twenty-first birthday and it was nice to be back home having a few pints with my Dad and a few pals and of course I soon lost track of time. Little did I know that the search parties were out and wondering where the hell I had go to.

Mr Revie had called the 'Boss' in Ipswich to see where I was as he thought I was on my way to Aberdeen and had no reason to think there was anything untoward occurring. The 'Boss' said he would get on the case and he telephoned my parents home in Carlisle to see if they had any news. I'm not sure what the reaction was when he was told by my Mum that I was in the pub with my old man. However he soon had John Carruthers – the scout who had originally sent me to Ipswich on trial around to see me and to find out what was going on.

There were also a number of family difficulties occurring at the time. My Mum had told me that they were about to be cut off by the electricity board as they had outstanding debts of nearly a hundred pounds, which they had no chance of paying. It was a lot of money back then and I was keen to help and gave her the money to sort things out. I know that my Mum appreciated having me around and with plenty on my mind, I told John that I was going nowhere and I stayed in the pub all night with my Dad and his pals when I should have been playing for my country. It wasn't a decision that I took lightly and in some ways I felt I was doing the honourable thing as my mind wasn't totally on the game.

Whilst I was in the pub in Carlisle, I had also been tracked down by the press pack, who had obviously been alerted as to what was a big story. They were very street-wise and aggressive and in the hope of getting rid of them, I gave them a few quotes, after which they asked me to pose for a photograph clutching a pint of lager in my hand. They also asked me to stand in front of a table, which was brimming with empty pint glasses, which were not all mine I might add. I obviously see the implications now, it looks like I'm something of a wastrel and I'm more interested in having a good night on the beer than I am in representing my country. I appreciate that I hadn't gone about things the right way, but I honestly thought that once I had explained my version of events then things would be fine.

I naively didn't see that there was any great problem or what the fuss was about. I hadn't realised that the press couldn't care less about me and I had now given them not only their back-page story but one for the front-page too. The enormity of what I had done only hit me the next day, as I was all over the national newspapers. The photograph of me standing over the beer looked horrendous and the accompanying article seemed to suggest that I had gone running home to my Mum. It also insinuated that I was an immature person, who clung onto her apron stings and that I wasn't able to accept my responsibilities either as a footballer or as a father to a small child of my own.

It was hurtful stuff and also less than complimentary about my parents and the fact that they couldn't afford to pay the outstanding bills. The only consolation was that I got a hundred quid out of one of the newspapers and gave it to my Mum. Though I was keen to tell her to keep that for herself and not tell my Dad about it, as it would have ended up getting spent in the pub. The reason I expect that they were in financial difficulty in the first place.

Upon my return to Ipswich, I immediately went to see the 'Boss,' who admitted that he was bewildered by my actions, but after speaking with him, he was very supportive and eventually

(top left)
The only official school
photograph of me. I was
rarely in the place.

(top right)
Getting married to my
beloved Maggie.

(left)
Desperate to make the grade in
my very first Ipswich Town kit.

A World Cup winner – part of the side which triumphed in the
'Little World Cup' held in 1972. I'm at the front wearing the shades.

Standing next to the great Sir Alf Ramsey as part of the England U-23 squad.
He told me I would have a long and illustrious international career.

I was known as Bobby Robson's 'tank' and was asked by the British Army if they could name a tank after me. How could I say no?

I was soon dubbed the new Bobby Moore
and the international caps began to accumulate.

saw why I had behaved as I had. I obviously also needed to speak with Don Revie although before I managed to call him, he had already sent me a telegram. It passed on his regards and that he hoped to see me playing again for England soon, which was very reassuring for me.

My non-appearance sparked something of a debate in the press, as it brought forward the question about the need for clubs to employ people who could help players cope with the increasing mental and psychological demands of the game. They are seen as a standard part of football these days, however back then, it was a new concept to think that the mental well being of a player might affect their performance on the park.

I eventually spoke to Mr Revie and I apologised about the Scotland debacle, I told him my reasons and he couldn't have been nicer about things. Mr Revie again reiterated how much he rated me and how he wanted me to play football for him. I was grateful for his understanding attitude and was determined to put things right. Especially when the 'Boss' and a few of the senior players at Ipswich, told me that I was worth much more than the detrimental headlines that I had inspired.

Shortly afterwards, I received another letter telling me that I was called up to play for the under-23 side against Wales at Vetch Field in Swansea. I was determined to put things right, especially when I was subjected to a few taunts of 'Beattie wants his Mummy,' from the Welsh contingent. In the end, I silenced them in the perfect way when I scored after twenty-seven minutes. I broke down a Welsh attack and went on a forward run which took me into the opposition half. Their defence kept backing away from me and when I got within striking distance, I let fly and drove the ball into the corner of the net. It was a sweet moment to have scored for my country, but it was extra special as I think it went some way to making amends for the Pittodrie fiasco. My club team-mate David Johnson added a second goal after sixty-eight minutes and we went on to enjoy a comfortable 2-0 victory.

Mr Revie was delighted, not only with my goal, but also with my overall performance. I know that we were both under scrutiny and that he had been criticised in some quarters, for selecting me so soon after the Scotland game. It was therefore good to stick up two fingers to all those who had been having a pop at us. My performance ensured that the newspapers also forgot about my previous indiscretion and the next morning produced headlines which I enjoyed reading, as they proclaimed: 'Ipswich 2 Wales 0.' They were complimentary about my reaction to events and my overall performance and it seemed that all was forgiven.

There had been calls before the game that I should never be picked at international level for the under-23 side again and following the game at Wales that proved to be the case. Although it was for good reasons, rather than as any punishment for my non-appearance, when a couple of months later I was called into the full England squad, for my debut in a European Championship qualifier against Cyprus.

I was again told via a letter sent to the club and when I saw the FA headed note paper I assumed I was being called up for another under-23 international. I was taken aback and had to read the letter a couple of times to make sure I hadn't made a mistake, but it was there in black and white. I had done it and was all set to receive the ultimate football accolade – a call up at full international level for my country. As before with my under-23 call up there were no nerves and I felt completely at home with it all. I was selected at left full-back, as opposed to my preferred central defensive position, which was a shame, but I would have played in goal if asked.

There were some terrific players in the team and I lined up alongside the likes of Kevin Keegan, Alan Ball and Colin Bell. We won the game 5-0 in a match made famous for the fact that Newcastle United striker Malcolm Macdonald scored all five goals. I actually scored in the game, but the goal was subsequently disallowed. I jabbed a loose ball into the net and at the same time, collided into the Cyprus 'keeper with my knee – ironically the same that was to cause me so many problems later in my career.

There was no malice intended and many, including myself, thought it was a harsh decision. As a result of the collision, the Cyprus 'keeper had to be replaced and his understudy was certainly no Gordon Banks. They were a poor side anyway and the substitute goalkeeper weakened them further. I don't wish to take anything away from 'Supermac' who I rated highly as a player, but I think the reserve 'keeper was awful and his inadequacies certainly helped him to notch his five goals.

I was on the England score-sheet myself a couple of months later when I scored in a magnificent 5-1 victory against Scotland at Wembley Stadium. It was part of the annual Home International fixtures and I really wanted to make my mark. I have Scottish ancestry and with Carlisle situated so close to the border between the two countries, I felt the rivalry more than most.

Despite the game being played at Wembley, there were plenty of Scotland supporters in the crowd, who of course gave us a lively welcome and were anxious to see us turned over. Fortunately we got off to the perfect start when Gerry Francis scored after only six minutes. Even better was to come when I soon notched a second goal for us.

It came following a Scottish attack when I headed away a ball which had been crossed into our penalty-area. Alan Ball picked up the loose ball and released Kevin Keegan, who started on a forward run. Following my clearance I had noticed there was nobody up-front, so I continued to steam forward the full-length of the pitch 'Six O'Clock Express' style and was picked out by a lovely cross-field pass by Kevin. The ball looped over to the far post where I beat the Scottish full-back Sandy Jardine in the air and headed the ball back over the Scottish 'keeper Stewart Kennedy, who in his endeavours to try and scramble back actually ran into the post.

I had scored for England at Wembley and fulfilled a boyhood dream in the process. We went on to totally overwhelm the Scottish side with Gerry Francis adding another and David Johnson and Colin Bell helping complete the rout. It made for a stunning afternoon's work and was my proudest moment in football to date.

It all helped cement another impressive season. We had come so close on the domestic front with Ipswich as not only did we reach the FA Cup semi-final, but we came third in the one of the closest league championships for many years. We finished only two points behind the eventual winners Derby County and actually won 23 games that season-two more than they had managed. Incredibly Burnley who had finished the season in tenth position, only finished a further six points behind us.

One or two silly results had cost us dearly, with the Carlisle game, one in particular that we should have won. I also felt that when we got one or two injuries, our squad did not have quite as much quality as that of our rivals. I did hear that the 'Boss' had wanted to strengthen the squad and sign one or two players with top class reputations. Names like Peter Shilton and Alan Ball were two that I heard mentioned. I also heard that he was interested in the Middlesbrough centre-half Willie Maddren, who would have kept me on my toes. However in the end, the board didn't have the money to fund the deals and so the transfers never materialised.

My own continued good form had not gone unnoticed at Ipswich Town and the 'Boss' called me in to his office to offer me a pay-rise. Although it has to be said, that contract negotiations then, were not what they are now. I went into his office and the 'Boss' told me that he was really pleased with me, 'What do you think you are worth son?' he asked me. I really had no idea and didn't have a clue what to say, so I just shrugged my shoulders. 'How does another fifty quid a week sound to you?' he said.

It sounded good to me and I duly signed up. This scenario would occur at the end of every season and I would always sign a new and improved four year contract. I never once questioned the amount offered and never thought to ask for any more. I genuinely loved playing football and it was never about money for me. I honestly couldn't believe I was getting paid to do something that I adored doing.

It was a lovely time to be at Ipswich, the club was run by the Cobbold family who were a distinguished group of people who had a lovely manner and a delightful sense of fun about them. The Chairman at the time was John Cobbold, known to all as Mr John. He once famously answered the question about whether there was a crisis at Ipswich Town, by saying that the only crisis he had encountered was when the boardroom had run out of white wine.

On another occasion, the Ipswich Town youngsters had won the FA Youth Cup and they held a celebration party at a local hotel. Mr John, no doubt fuelled by a glass or two of bubbly got up to give a speech to the audience. People were expecting a series of formal comments but Mr John brought the house down, when he demanded that the parents return to their rooms: 'In order to create another winning side for us.'

On one of our mid-season breaks, Mr John accompanied us to Kuwait – which as a predominantly Muslim country, obviously meant that alcohol was forbidden. Mr John was renowned for enjoying a tipple and the lads were also ready to let off some steam, so we were not going to let anything stop us having some fun. We bought a huge quantity of booze in the duty free lounge in the UK and placed the bottles into the club training kit basket. Everything was running smoothly until we pushed it over the tiled airport floor in Kuwait, where you could hear the bottles rattling.

I began whistling to drown out the noise and although we got one or two funny looks we were allowed through. We eventually found some British lads who knew all the secret drinking haunts, so we really needn't have bothered, although the booze became a bit of an earner for us, as an Arab we met in the hotel bought it from us for £50 a bottle. It was a good deal, as the same stuff had only cost us a fiver back in the UK.

On another trip abroad to Canada, I took the opportunity to buy some Beattie tartan and got a kilt made up from it. When I arrived back in England, I wore it to an official club function. Mr John soon approached and I thought I might be in for a telling off, however, he had a huge grin on his face and declared that he wanted to wear the kilt and I was happy to oblige. Later after he'd had a few drinks he lifted it up to reveal to all, 'What a real man wears under his kilt.'

The 'Boss' also provided us with some humorous moments, although not always intentionally. He is of course famed for getting players names wrong and occasionally jumbling sentences up so that they mean something quite different. 'Do well today and you can have two days off tomorrow,' is one that I remember.

On another occasion, the team had all been invited to play golf and the 'Boss' was so wrapped up in his conversation that he actually walked into a bunker and collapsed in a heap covered in sand. That was the kind of atmosphere I was involved with on a daily basis. We had a great side on the park and a great time away from things and it was a pleasure and a privilege to be there.

I was to make an unexpected return to Anfield when I was asked by Bill Shankly to play in his testimonial game. Although I had played there before, it was always a strange feeling returning to Anfield and in many ways I was surprised he wanted me to play. However, I received a warm welcome from him and he told me there were no hard feelings. He said that he wanted the best players in the country on the park and that in his opinion I was one of them.

'I haven't made many mistakes son, but letting you get away was one of them,' he added. It was a great compliment from a great football man and one which I treasured. I would have loved to have played football for him, as the Liverpool side of that era were terrific. However I was enjoying life at Ipswich Town and had made the England team so I had no regrets.

It was an emotional evening and at the end Mr Shankly presented me with an envelope as a payment for attending. I didn't want anything and refused to take it, it was fantastic to be part of such a fabulous occasion and that was payment enough. However he insisted, 'Take it son, I've made a few bob tonight,' he said. Inside was £50, although I wish I had received a trophy, or some kind of memento, especially as I spent most of the money on the way home.

At the start of the 1975/6 season, I continued where I had left off and I was called in to see the 'Boss' who informed me that I had been named the Daily Mirror player of the month. I was later presented with the award before a game by none other than Sir Alf Ramsey, who told me how pleased he was with my progress. He obviously still had a strong sense of affection for Ipswich Town and he told me how he always looked out for the team's results and kept an eye on my performances. It was another in a long list of wonderful accolades.

I subsequently had one of the more unusual arrive when I received a letter from Major Stanley Manthorpe of the 2nd Royal tank regiment, who asked if I would give my permission to let the regiment name an 80ft Chieftain tank after me. The letter arrived care of the club, so as with my initial under-23 call up, I thought that it was somebody winding me up. However it was found to be a legitimate request and one which I couldn't possibly turn down.

The letter went on to explain that it was an event inspired after I had played during a televised game, when I gave a full-blooded performance, which had the 'Boss' saying that I was his own 'Private tank.' Apparently some of the army lads based in Germany picked up on this and they asked Major Manthorpe if he would get in touch with me. I was more than happy to agree and a tank was brought over to the ground at Portman Road and I climbed on board for a series of photographs.

Later in the season I got the chance to visit the lads and upon my arrival, I was taken to the parade ground where situated was the tank with my name emblazoned down the side. I've always enjoyed cars and bikes and so to get the chance to drive this fifty ton beast was a great thrill. The army lads were a great bunch and great hosts, who loved their football and I signed autographs until my arm ached. Afterwards I was taken to their private quarters and it's fair to say that the booze flowed. The whole occasion was a very humbling experience for me but a hugely enjoyable one all the same.

Later on that season, I got something else to drive around in when a couple of lads from a local garage offered me a deal to provide me with a sponsored car. They seemed like a decent bunch that enjoyed their football and after going out for a few lunches with them I felt I had nothing to lose by accepting the offer.

On the face of things, it seemed too good to be true, a free car and all I had to do was allow them to have a logo that put my name – as sponsored by the name of their company down the side of the vehicle. A week later my new vehicle arrived, although as well as the agreed logo down the side, I noticed that it also had a caricature painting of someone painted on the bonnet. I wasn't sure who it was, but then someone piped up that it was a caricature of me. I would never have guessed and in all honesty it looked like a five-year old had drawn it. It was supposed to provide things with a touch of glamour, but in reality it made my new car look like an ice-cream van. I wasn't convinced at all, but then I figured as the car was for free it would be ungrateful to complain too much. It definitely ensured that I turned a few heads whilst buzzing around town and such a unique looking vehicle meant that any sort of anonymity was over. I had my fair share of autograph hunters in those days, which was always fine with me, but I now found that no matter where I parked the car, whenever I returned there was always a group of people there waiting for me. As the saying goes 'Nothing attracts a crowd, like a crowd' and I would often return to my vehicle and find literally dozens of people there. This would even occur when I had made a trip to my local shop for a newspaper and a packet of cigarettes.

One afternoon I arrived at Portman Road in the car before a home fixture versus Liverpool and was immediately approached by two guys who I assumed were supporters after an autograph. I was therefore surprised when they identified themselves as police officers. I wasn't sure what was happening, but apparently they wanted to speak to me about the lads at the garage who had sponsored my car.

I wasn't sure why and with a football game to play, I had better things on my mind. However it was an order rather than an invitation, so I went to the police station after the game to make a statement. I had absolutely no idea what it was all about, but upon my arrival, the police officers informed me that the lads at the garage were under arrest and that they had been taping all the telephone calls they had made over the last few months. They had also been following them around, as well as placing the garage under twenty-four hour observation and anyone who had been in any sort of contact had been pulled in to explain themselves.

It turned out that the lads had been buying large properties in the countryside and then insuring the places to the maximum amount and setting them on fire to claim on the insurance. Of course I knew nothing about this and said as much to the police, who were happy with my version of events. However they went on to explain the whole tangled web to me before I was let out to go on my way.

It turned out that the police had been made aware that something untoward was occurring, when an off duty police officer had spotted the infamous gangster Charlie Kray arriving at Ipswich train station. It is a small town and so somebody with his reputation was bound to attract attention. The officer decided to follow him and he went straight to see the lads at the garage.

Kray ended up staying in Ipswich for a few days and was never out of their company, so they began bugging 'phones and obviously the lads would ring me from time to time to ask about the car and to chat generally about football and the like. Apparently dozens of people who had even the most tenuous of connections with the lads were dragged in, as the case was eventually very big news and the police wanted to ensure that they rounded everybody up.

The lads at the garage were eventually given hefty prison sentences and whilst they were on remand at Norwich prison, I went to visit one of them. The 'Boss' hadn't said much until this point, but it was a different story when he found out about my visit. One of the screws had seen me and tipped him off saying that I had been visiting 'heavy duty gangsters,' which in hindsight they maybe were.

However they had been good to me and never involved me in their activities, so that is all I was concerned about. Although I did decide it was best if I curtailed my visits, as I was only bound to attract bad publicity for myself. I had continued to be selected for England and the last thing I needed was the newspapers getting hold of the story.

After the distraction of the car scenario, it was good to get back to concentrating on football. Although I was thrilled to be getting picked for my country, historically it was not the greatest time to be an England player. The glory years of the Sir Alf Ramsey era were over and as a country we had failed to qualify for the 1974 World Cup.

The appointment of Don Revie as national team manager eventually proved to be a controversial one and as a man he wasn't universally popular. I personally liked the man and remained grateful to him for not only being so understanding about my disappearing act in the under-23 game, but also for giving me my debut at full international level.

I think that he always tried to do the right thing, although unfortunately for him it didn't always work out. A good example of this came after Mr Revie had invited practically every decent player who was English to a weekend get-together. I can remember turning up and there seemed to be dozens of footballers there ranging from seasoned internationals through to inexperienced players. I honestly didn't think that there would be enough room for us all in the hotel.

There was no reason for us to be there and there wasn't really anything for us to do, it was just Mr Revie's way of sending out an all-inclusive message, saying that everyone was in his thoughts. Instead it left many feeling confused and others said it devalued the meaning of what an England international footballer meant.

I was still getting used to being fortunate enough to be staying in fancy hotels and having access to things like room-service, so in many ways the only memorable event for me was the food which was superb. I tried smoked salmon for the first time and during my stay subsequently ate it for my breakfast, lunch and evening meal.

Whenever we were on international duty Mr Revie would hand out a dossier of information on the opposition, which I suppose illustrated incredible detail on his part and again may have been seen as an example of him wanting an all-inclusive atmosphere. However like a lot of other players, I found the dossiers confusing and also boring. I was proud to be there and ready to give my all, and whilst I was never big-headed enough to think I knew everything, I personally think the dossiers were the wrong way to go about helping me do my job.

In all honesty, I was never really one for team-talks, I felt that the game was decided on the pitch and not in the dressing-room and I just liked to get out there and get on with it. I wasn't being arrogant, I just found it boring listening to endless discussions about what might happen. I wanted to get out there where it actually did happen.

I remember at Ipswich, the 'Boss' pretty much gave up on giving me any kind of advice and just left me alone. Whilst he spoke to everyone else, I often used to disappear and have a cigarette, or sit on the toilet and read the match-day programme. I always did the business for him on the pitch and so he realised that saying anything to me was a waste of his time and he might as well direct his energy into someone who would benefit from his advice. This was what I had being used to and so unfortunately and with no disrespect meant to Mr Revie, my dossier ended up in the bin.

There were of course some tremendous players in the England squad, Kevin Keegan, Colin Bell and Alan Ball were players who stood out for me. Alan brought his World Cup winners medal to show me which was a great inspiration, as I wanted one of my own. Colin and Kevin were also good guys and I got on well with them, although they couldn't quite understand how I managed to smoke so many cigarettes and still play to such a high standard of football. As with any football team there are also those who are great characters and I ended up rooming with one of the most madcap of all – Manchester United winger Gordon Hill.

I remember that on one international call-up, Mr Revie had given us the opportunity to have a day off and I accompanied Gordon to the cinema and on the way there we bought a gorilla mask each. When we arrived Gordon made a point of deliberately visiting an X-rated film, which was being watched by a room full of the dirty-mack brigade. Gordon proceeded to don his mask and he wandered up to these blokes, who were looking pretty embarrassed anyway dressed up as gorilla. I figured it seemed like good fun, so I soon joined in.

It obviously put them off enjoying the film and when one or two started getting angry, we decided to leave. It was only when we got back to the team hotel that I realised what a scandal we could have caused. I am sure that the News of the World would have loved to have found out about the two England footballers, wearing gorilla masks, wandering about a cinema showing a porno film.

It didn't immediately sink in though and when we got back to the hotel we proceeded to do the same, jumping out of wardrobes and the like, and frightening the lads half to death as nobody was quite sure who it was underneath the gorilla masks. However there was no fooling big Joe Corrigan, who had been around the block and knew that only Gordon and I would be daft enough to get up to such antics. When we jumped out in front of him, he didn't bat an eyelid, even though we were still wearing our masks, he knew it was us straight away and so we had to look elsewhere for our fun.

The next morning we went outside the hotel, where there was a lake with several rowing boots moored by a small jetty. Every morning Mr Revie's assistant – Les Cocker, used to jump into one of the boats and row up and down the lake. Before he arrived, Gordon and I tied a rope to the plug situated in the bottom of the boat and hid behind some nearby trees and when Les jumped in and started rowing, we literally pulled the plug on him.

Les crashed into the water and whilst Gordon and I were in fits of laughter, he began flapping his arms around and screaming out that he couldn't swim. We soon realised that our prank had turned sour and I stripped off and jumped into the water to save him. As I was wading further into the water, I noticed that it wasn't getting any deeper and as I approached Les, he merely stood up and walked away laughing. It turned out that the lake was about three-feet deep. Les had found out about our prank and turned the tables on us.

Despite this and despite Gordon's best efforts – communicating only in the style of Norman Wisdom, who was a big star back then, it wasn't always a happy camp. Kevin Keegan actually walked out during one training session only to return for a game against Czechoslovakia and it seemed that the national game was in a period of transition. Mr Revie had a tough act to follow in Sir Alf Ramsey and it really did seem that whatever he did, it ended in controversy and as a result, he was doomed to failure as the England manager.

He actually engineered a deal with a well known football boot manufacturer which ensured we got £300 if we wore a pair whilst on international duty. The match fee for playing for England in those days was £100, so he probably thought he was doing us a favour. Instead it stirred up a lot of antagonism amongst certain players who felt that playing for your country was an honour and money should not be an issue. This in itself I suppose is incredible as footballers are and always have been accused of being greedy.

I personally have to say that I could see both sides of the argument. Money was the last thing on my mind when I pulled on that famous white jersey and I would have personally paid money to have played, never mind being bothered about someone paying me. On the other hand I was still mindful of how hard money could be to come across.

It was still only a few years since I had been living in Carlisle when I wasn't always guaranteed so much as a hot meal at the end of my working day. In many ways I think the whole situation illustrated that Mr Revie was always going to find it tough to be the England manager. At Leeds United I believe he had a very loyal team of players who idolised him. It was obviously a different scenario at England level and I wasn't surprised his reign ended prematurely.

With regard to the boots, I did actually wear them, but after a couple of games they felt uncomfortable, so I wore my usual boots with the sponsors logo stuck over the top. I know a few other lads did this, so we basically earned £300 for nothing. This would have been unthinkable to me a few years previously and whilst footballer players now earn a lot more money than I ever did, I realised that I was moving into another league financially.

It became clear how much, when on one England trip we went for a day to the races. Mick Channon had heard a whisper for a horse and told the lads it was a sure thing and worth 'Five apiece.' Mick was obviously a shrewd judge and I was happy to hand him a fiver. When I did, he looked at me as if I was some sort of idiot, I soon realised why as Mick meant five hundred. There was no way I was having five hundred pounds on a horse and so I left it at a fiver. In the end Mick proved why he has gone on to become a successful race-horse trainer and left me wishing I had put five hundred on, as the horse duly romped home.

Making the breakthrough into the full international side was undoubtedly the highlight of this period of my career, as on the domestic front with Ipswich Town we never really looked like winning anything. In 1975/6, we finished sixth in the league and our best run on the cup front took us only as far as the fourth round of the FA Cup, where we eventually bowed out against Wolverhampton Wanderers following a replay.

Despite the relative disappointment of the season, we had established a reputation as being a very useful side that played a style of football which was easy on the eye. The 'Boss' always had us well organised and made sure we prepared well and that I always did my homework on opposing strikers as to their particular strengths and weaknesses, although my preparation was somewhat disrupted during one game away at Leeds United.

About ten minutes before the kick-off, Leeds winger Eddie Gray came running over and told me that my Dad had turned up and was going to chin the Leeds commissionaire because he wouldn't let him into the players lounge. No one could calm my Dad down and I was asked to go and sort things out, even though at the time I was in my kit and ready to go onto the pitch for the game.

It turned out that my Dad had made an impromptu visit to Elland Road and didn't have a ticket. He thought that by merely telling the guy at the main reception that I was his son, it would be enough to get him invited in. When of course it wasn't, he decided to go ballistic. Fortunately I managed to calm him down and sort things out and was able to get on with playing football.

Ironically after the game, I went into the players lounge and the first people who I saw were my Dad and the commissionaire. They were sat in a corner of the room, having a drink together as if they the best of pals, when it had only been a couple of hours earlier that my Dad was going to pull his head off. Also there with my Dad was Robin Turner's Father. Robin – a striker at the club also hailed from Carlisle, so the two old boys had travelled down together. As things had seemingly calmed down I joined them for a drink and before I departed back to Ipswich, I slipped my Dad a few quid for the journey home and Robin did the same for his old man.

A few days later, I 'phoned home and my Mum answered and after a general chat, I asked her if Dad had enjoyed the game. 'I wouldn't know son,' she replied, 'He hasn't arrived back home yet.' Apparently my Dad and Robin's old man were still AWOL, although it wasn't the first time this had happened, nor was it the last and so my Mum wasn't too worried.

I waited another few days and called back to see if everything was ok. I again spoke to my Mum and it turned that my Dad had only just arrived home. Along with Robin's old man, they had ended up in Edinburgh and had stayed there, before eventually making it home nearly a week after they both originally should have been back.

SECOND-HALF

It was towards the end of the season that I began to suffer the first injury problems of my career. Up until then it had been something of a fairytale: plucked from obscurity, first-team at Ipswich, PFA award, England international recognition. The only blot on my copybook was the Scotland no-show. I began to experience severe back pain, which I couldn't understand, as I hadn't taken a knock or had anything untoward occur. After a series of tests, it was eventually diagnosed as damage to the sacroiliac joint. Essentially they are two joints which are situated at the base of the spine, which are attached to the pelvis. Nobody could understand what had caused the problem although all I knew was that I was in agony and was limping around like an old man.

There wasn't much anyone could do, which was very worrying and nobody knew what I could do to rectify the situation. In the end I began working with the club physiotherapist, who used to lay me on the floor and manipulate the area in question and practically push it back into place, as the problem apparently stemmed from the joint coming out of the socket. Fortunately it did the trick, although I was told that I would always have a problem and it was something I would have to contend with.

I believe that it could have been attributed to an early incident when as a youngster. I had helped my Dad when he worked delivering coal and can remember one morning I was lugging bags of coal around and then feeling the most tremendous pain in my back. I had obviously done some kind of damage, although

The Greatest Footballer England Never Had

nobody could ever work out what had happened, as like most back injuries it was very difficult to diagnose and also remedy.

The pain eventually went away, although it appeared that it had returned due to the physical demands of my life as a professional footballer. Someone told me I should try some stretching exercises as it might help, so each day I began spending time hanging from the crossbar on the training pitch. It amused a few of the lads, although I have to say it helped temporarily sort things out and ease my pain which was fine by me.

Whilst I was the recipient of some good natured banter from the lads at Ipswich, I continued to attract the plaudits from those outside the club. This certainly helped my spirits and helped keep me going following my injury woes. Some of the nicer compliments were bestowed on me after the disappointment of failing to qualify for the 1974 World Cup. Attention soon turned to the 1978 campaign and I was strongly fancied to be the man who would captain the side and many people within football and the media were saying as much. In fact some were suggesting it was a formality and that I would be the bedrock of the England side for many years to come.

The start of the 1976/77 season at Ipswich Town, saw us kick off proceedings with some excellent results, we beat Liverpool and Manchester United and soon equalled our club record score, when during one fixture we thumped West Bromwich Albion by seven goals to nil. I had a great game and even scored with a beauty, when I thumped a long-range effort past John Osborne, who later joked that he was pleased that he hadn't got a hand to the ball as it would have knocked it clean off.

The 'Boss' added a touch of class during that season, when he signed Paul Mariner from Plymouth. He was an excellent player, as well as a great character and we got on well personally. Not long after his arrival we were out having a drink in the town, when we bumped into a couple of other guys who introduced themselves. One was a bookmaker, whilst the other owned amusement arcades, so we were in the company of gamblers and we soon had a card school on the go.

I was honestly never much of a gambler, but on this occasion I seemed to have lady luck on my side and I was soon several hundred pounds up. The bookmaker seemed to be chasing his losses and as is often the case began digging a bigger hole for himself. He soon put a set of keys on the table and told me he was willing to put up one of his shops. It was getting heavy, but I was a mile in front money-wise at this stage so I figured I had nothing to lose.

We flipped the cards and I had won. The guy left the keys on the table and with nothing more said he walked away. The next day I went to the betting shop and I was about to put the key in the lock when the door pushed open by itself. Inside was an empty shop, it turned out that the bookie had gone bust and my winning prize was utterly worthless.

A nicer memory I associate with 'PM,' came as a result of the constant ribbing I received from the 'Boss' over getting my hair cut. It was one of the few things I ignored him over, as I was a rocker at heart and so kept my hair long, which was very much in vogue at the time. Once I was near the offices by the side of the club and heard the 'Boss,' shout out half jokingly, 'Get that bloody hair cut Beattie,' however he wasn't shouting at me, he was shouting at someone else.

The other guy looked a bit bemused to say the least and then I saw the 'Boss' apologising profusely to him as he realised his mistake. I looked over and the recipient of the telling-off looked familiar and so I went over to introduce myself. We shook hands and he told me his name and then it became apparent why I had recognised his face. It turned out the long-haired mystery man, was none other than Ian Gillan, the lead singer of Deep Purple who had come to see Paul Mariner who was a good friend of his. I'm not sure what he made of it all, but he seemed to take it in good spirits and we had a good laugh about it all. It was a strange time, as I can remember playing a game at Newcastle United, which we were losing. The weather was atrocious and eventually the game was abandoned. The Geordie fans were outraged, as not only were their side in front, but it was also a wasted Saturday afternoon for them.

I am not sure we would have got anything out of the game, so I was pleased to have been given a reprieve. I was especially pleased, when I returned to the dressing room and found that we had been given a complimentary barrel of Newcastle Brown Ale which we proceeded to polish off on the long journey home.

The bad weather conditions reminded me of an earlier game when we had played at Burnley, it absolutely poured down with rain and the pitch resembled a paddy-field. We eventually got a penalty, which I stepped up to take, although I had to place the ball on a mound of mud as it would have literally sunk. When the penalty was eventually taken, it was not only the ball that went towards goal, but also the huge mound of mud. Burnley 'keeper Alan Stevenson was obviously confused, as he dived one way and saved the mud, whilst the ball went flying in the opposite direction and into the net.

The season was one where I had hoped to re-establish myself back in the England team as I had to pull out of several squads due to my back problems. However any hope I had of doing so, were abandoned towards the end of the season. Things ended prematurely for me following a serious accident, which still has people asking me what happened almost three decades later. It occurred when my father in-law gave me an old tin barrel to burn the leaves and rubbish that were accumulating in my garden. One afternoon I set to work and began loading them into the barrel and proceeded to get a fire going, I left it for a while and attended to other things in the garden and then went back and noticed that the fire in the barrel had gone out. In order to stoke it up, I went into the garage where I always kept a can of petrol. I tipped some petrol into the barrel and the next thing a huge flame shot up which blasted into my in the face. I staggered backwards, as my hair had now caught fire and I ran into the house and managed to grab a towel which I frantically ran under the tap and then placed over my face and head in order to put out the flames.

I knew I needed to get to the hospital, but I didn't want Maggie to see me, especially as she was eight months pregnant at the time, so I tried to cover my face with the towel, which had the effect of frightening her even more. I eventually got her to get my next door neighbour and in his rush to get me to the hospital, he made matters worse when he smashed my new Rover car, which was my pride and joy at the time into a wall. He eventually got me to the hospital, where I was immediately placed in a special unit. As if my injuries weren't enough to be worrying about, the rumour mill kicked into full effect and the tabloids soon had a story that Maggie and myself had been arguing and that my injuries had come as a result of her throwing a chip-pan full of hot oil over me.

Whilst I was in hospital, Maggie had to be looked after by her family, which was just as well as reporters were sniffing around the house and wouldn't take no for an answer. Apparently they were shining a searchlight into the house trying to look in and see what was going on. In the end Maggie's Dad had to call the police to come and get rid of them. There was one newspaper that was particularly aggressive about the whole thing and I won't so much as have a copy of it in the house today.

There was also something of a furore when the district health administrator made an out of office statement to the press about the nature of my injuries. This contravened union rules and also my right to a degree of confidentiality and there were suggestions that I should sue. I was tempted, but I felt that I had enough to contend with my injuries and so whilst I wasn't happy, I decided to let things go.

My injuries were not good – in particular the ones to my neck, which had bore the brunt of the blast and they were made worse by the fact that a piece of the nylon t-shirt I was wearing at the time had melted there. The 'Boss' came to see me and I told him not to worry and that I would be fit for the following game. He had an anxious look on his face and told me to get better in my own time. I hadn't appreciated the extent of my injuries and didn't play for the rest of the season, so the 'Boss' had obviously seen straight away how serious it all was.

Ironically whilst I recuperated in hospital, one of the nurses asked if I would go see the other patients and sign a few autographs. One of them was a lady who actually had been scalded by hot chip pan oil, as apparently she had tried to throw a pan that was on fire out of the window and the wind blew it all back over her. I looked at her and thanked God that it wasn't a fate I had suffered and it was only a rumour, as she was laid prostrate on the bed, could hardly speak and looked like a piece of charcoal. I wasn't feeling the greatest at this time myself, however, having seen her I realised that it could have been much worse. Although if I thought I was feeling somewhat uncomfortable then, a few days after the accident it all got much worse.

When someone is burned the area is essentially numbed, so the pain is just about bearable. However as the damaged nerves begin to repair, the pain intensifies and it soon became intolerable for me. The only trouble was that nobody had told me and I was literally screaming in agony and had to be pumped full of morphine to help me cope with it all.

I had burns on my face but the wound on my neck was particularly nasty and I feared I would be scarred for life. Fortunately the hospital had been experimenting with a new spray which had first been used on burns victims in the Vietnam War. It delivered great results and luckily it had the desired effect as apart from a very small mark you wouldn't know I'd had any problems if you saw me today.

Unfortunately if the burns have faded the rumours haven't, I can be out somewhere today, almost thirty years later and without fail, someone will stop me and quiz me about 'What really happened?' or else pass comment on how well I'm looking for someone who has had a chip pan full of hot oil thrown over them.

As I was not playing much football, I had plenty of time on my hands and was often down at the club trying to get myself fit. There was a young lad who was always hanging around and eventually he became a ball-boy at the club. I was a bit of a hero to him and as he was a nice polite lad, we got on well. We kept in touch and a few years later I was thrilled to be watching him on the television. Only now he wasn't a ball-boy but a darts player.

The lad in question was Keith Deller, who eventually won the World Darts Championship when he beat Eric Bristow in the final. Fast forward a few years later and Keith was to come to my assistance. When David Beckham was at Manchester United and scored his famous goal against Wimbledon from inside his own half, a number of pundits were claiming it was the first time that this had happened.

I don't know if anyone else had managed it, but I know that I had done it during a game against Leeds United. I spotted their 'keeper off his line and figured I would have a go and then saw the ball sail over the stranded David Harvey into the top corner of the net. Keith had been at the game and had got in touch with the people at the BBC to tell them that not only had I achieved the same feat, but I had done it a good twenty years before Mr Beckham had managed to do so.

By the start of the 1977/8 season I was raring to go and I was keen to put all my injury and accident worries behind me, I had missed a lot of football and was keen to make amends, although I came back into an Ipswich Town side that was not at its best. Our early form was patchy, best summed up when we suffered a conclusive defeat against high-flying Nottingham Forest who thrashed us 4-0. On a personal note, I soon got back into the swing of things and my form was good and I was delighted to be called into an England squad to face Luxembourg in a mid-week game at Wembley.

On the Saturday before the international, my run of bad luck continued when I injured my knee in a league fixture against West Bromwich Albion. I knew something was wrong but I tried to shrug off the pain and carry on playing. After the game the knee was still giving me problems and I probably should have pulled out of the England squad which was only three days later, but I was determined to regain my international place, as I was totally sick of life on the sidelines.

In the end it was decided that it was best I sit on the bench as the knee didn't feel right and I knew something was wrong. Although I did make an appearance late in the game which in hindsight wasn't the best idea as my knee required a period of rest. After the game the medical staff investigated and the prognosis was not good. It was decided that I needed an operation as my cartilage was damaged and I went into hospital shortly afterwards.

I subsequently had the cartilage removed and was back home within a couple of days. Recovery time from operations of this nature varied, but it was thought that I would be out for quite some time. Following the problems with my back and the fire, I was absolutely gutted but I amazed everyone when I returned within three weeks in time for a crunch fixture for Ipswich Town against Barcelona in the UEFA Cup.

I worked hard to regain my fitness and mobility and in order to null the pain in my knee, I played with the aid of a cortisone injection, which I was happy to have administered. Quite frankly anything that allowed me to play football was fine by me. All I wanted to do was play and it was great to be back, especially as we subsequently took a Barcelona side, featuring Johan Cruyff, apart when we recorded a stunning 3-0 victory. It was a great team performance and one of the best during my time at the club as Mr Cruyff hardly got a kick all evening.

I had hoped that I was now back on track and the atmosphere around the club following such a great evening's work was wonderful. However the following day I felt a different emotion – namely one of intense pain, as my knee was very swollen and

I could hardly walk. I continued to attend training sessions but after any exertion my knee subsequently never felt right enough to play in formal games. There was talk of another operation and rumours that I had not done myself any favours by coming back so soon to play in the Barcelona game. However if asked again I would have played in that or any other match.

Any further operation was put on hold, as like any club in those days, we didn't have a large squad to pick from and I wanted to be around to play my part as often as I could. It was especially important as it was shaping up to be a huge season for us, as whilst our form in the league remained patchy, we were still involved in both the FA and UEFA Cup respectively.

I didn't want to miss out and wanted to play and I informed the club that I would play on one leg if necessary. It was decided that I would be wrapped up in cotton-wool and would play as and when crunch games arrived. It was for that reason I didn't play in the return leg at Barcelona. As with a 3-0 advantage from the first leg it was felt that we had done enough to not need to risk playing me. Instead I travelled with the squad in order to lend moral support.

I have never been the best at watching football and this evening was particularly painful. There was nothing I could do except sit and suffer, as I watched Johan Cruyff turn on a master-class as Barcelona proceeded to win the game 3-0. As the game was now level on aggregate, it went to a penalty shoot-out and my agony was complete when we eventually lost that to crash out of the tie altogether. Afterwards the 'Boss' said that he thought we would have held out, had I been on the park. I believe he intended it as a compliment, but to be honest it made me feel even more frustrated.

Even though I didn't play I still made the national newspapers the following day. The club press officer – a good friend of mine called Mel Henderson, had been approached by a Spanish newspaper about getting a couple of photographs with a famous Spanish actress and one of the Ipswich Town footballers. It seemed harmless enough stuff and as I wasn't playing I seemed the perfect person to use for the shots.

I subsequently arranged to meet her and arrived in the lobby with Mel, where we were met by the actress, who I thought must be doing well for herself as she was a wearing an expensive looking full-length fur coat. She was surrounded by photographers who were obviously ready to go to work and she seemed to be a big star. I introduced myself and as I sat myself down on a nearby chair, the actress suddenly leapt forward and sat herself on my knee. Her fur coat had gone, and all she was wearing underneath was an all in one fishnet stocking.

She suddenly started kissing me and I could hear a crescendo of cameras clicking and with that she was off my knee, the fur coat was back on and she had gone. In my younger days I wouldn't have complained about such a short and sweet experience, but I was now a married man and knew that any photographs wouldn't necessarily be telling the full story of what happened. I also didn't fancy having to explain myself to Maggie for something that I hadn't actually instigated.

I was reassured by Mel that the pictures were for the Spanish market only and whilst I didn't necessarily like been taken advantage of, I thought that there wasn't much I could do about it, so we left it at that. I was therefore horrified on my return to the UK to notice that the photographs were plastered all over the newspapers. One of which was underneath a headline which said: 'What's

Spanish for stop it lady, I'm married?' If that wasn't bad enough, it emerged that the actress was a woman called Susannah Estrada and the only acting she had done, was work which had made her Spain's foremost porno star.

I thought that this was the sort of thing that could only happen to me and I knew I had a lot of explaining to do. I wasn't looking forward to having to explain myself to Maggie, even though I hadn't done anything wrong. In the end when we arrived back in the UK, I had to get the 'Boss' and Mel to come straight over to my home and say that it wasn't my fault and I had been stitched up and fortunately everything soon got smoothed over.

The Barcelona fiasco was somewhat indicative of the season as a whole. I was still unable to play and the season seemed to be going nowhere and I was helpless to watch as the club continued to struggle in the league. Barcelona had obviously ended our UEFA Cup hopes and soon the only thing we were playing for was the FA Cup – not that I was playing too much at this time due to my various injury woes.

The early years of my career had seemed very easy and I didn't handle the setbacks well. I found it hard to cope with the long endless days of nothing that stretched out before me, as I have never been the type of person who had a hobby or particularly enjoyed sitting around the house. I tried having a round of golf, or going for a walk in order to keep me occupied, however I was soon feeling restless as all I wanted to do was play football.

I was desperate to get back on the pitch and I managed to come back for the fourth round of the FA Cup for a fairly straight forward win against Hartlepool. However each game that I played in involved a cortisone injection, which got me through the game but left me in agony afterwards. My frustration was intensified, as our form in the league was bad and we looked like relegation candidates.

There was no way that I was going to sit idle as the club slid out of the league and I continued to play as much as I could and was happy to help the cause, even though I knew that after the games I would be in pain. Fortunately we gathered enough points to help us stay afloat and even better was the fact that we had kept the FA Cup run going and we found ourselves in the semi-final against West Bromwich Albion which was played at Highbury. When I was given the all clear to play, I was determined not to go out at this stage again.

The game was an intense affair, as I think it's the old cliché of no one wanting to miss out on a final appearance. In those days it was without doubt the showpiece game of the season and everyone who was a football fan harboured dreams of being able to play in a final. I have to say that the appointment of Clive Thomas as the referee was not one that I welcomed, although it didn't matter as we got off to a terrific start when Brian Talbot put us in front after twelve minutes with a bullet header. Although the goal was marred by Brian having to leave the pitch with a head injury as in his endeavours to score he had clashed heads with Albion defender John Wile.

When Mick Mills scored eight minutes later, I knew it would be our day, as it wasn't often Mick got on the score-sheet. We seemed in control and myself and Allan Hunter had kept their strikers Cyrille Regis and Alistair Brown quiet and we were cruising to victory, when they scored from a penalty. It made for a nervous few minutes but John Wark popped up with a headed goal and at 3-1 up I knew that we were through.

We had played really well and in the end we were worthy

winners. I was finally going to fulfil every schoolboy's dream and play in an FA Cup final. However my mood soon changed, when the following day my knee was again horribly swollen and I began to realise I wasn't a certainty to play. I was getting fed-up with the same rigmarole and I longed for the days when I played week in, week out. I was only twenty-five years of age at this point and following a game I was often left hobbling around like someone who was three times that age.

My mind was temporarily taken off things, when I received an approach from the legendary ticket tout Stan Flashman. With an impending FA Cup final, it didn't take a genius to work out why he was calling. The players were expecting about twenty tickets each from the club, so imagine my surprise when we were told that we were getting six times that amount – each.

I quickly made contact with Stan and was told to report to his office in London, which was near to King's Cross station in London and it was then that I began to realise what I had got myself into. I walked up several flights of stairs and the nearer I got to the top, the more nervous I got. Eventually I reached the top-floor and there stood this enormous guy who was clearly Stan's bodyguard. He said nothing and merely stepped out of the way, so I continued on further down the corridor and eventually came across two even bigger guys – which was some feat in itself, who stood in front of what was presumably Stan's office.

I was feeling distinctly uncomfortable at this point and wasn't sure what I'd let myself in for. 'I'm here to see Mr Flashman' I said meekly. 'We know,' one of them barked. He glared at me aggressively and eventually stepped aside. I was here to do Stan a favour and had been invited over, so I shudder to think what reaction someone who owed him money or had done him a bad turn would have got.

I went in to see Stan and all I wanted to do was to give him his tickets and be on my way. He was a big man and was sat behind an even bigger desk which was covered with boxes of tickets. It was rumoured that for the right price he could get you a ticket for one of the Queen's tea parties at Buckingham Palace and I've no doubt that he could.

Stan was perfectly pleasant and he seemed pleased to see me, he wanted to talk about football and was a big West Ham fan. His hero was Bobby Moore and as a number of people had done in the past, he likened me to the great man. To be honest, I wasn't really listening as I just wanted to get the hell out of there.

Coming from a council estate, I have met my fair share of hard-cases and they have never bothered me, but I knew that Stan was on another level and I was very wary of him. I was eventually given a briefcase and thankfully I was on my way. On my out, the bodyguard again stepped out of the way and as he did this, his jacket rose up. There in his inside pocket was a gun, I was renowned for my speed on the football pitch, but I don't think I've ever moved as fast as I did that day.

I immediately went to the station and jumped on the first train back to Ipswich. It wasn't until I got home that I bothered to check the contents of the briefcase. I threw the case on my bed and opened it up and then I counted the money and it came to £36,000, which was a colossal amount and certainly more than I had ever seen.

By now it was late and I had no alternative but to put the money back in the case and stick it in the loft. I didn't sleep very well and was terrified that I might be attacked during the night. Fortunately nothing happened and the next day I took it to the ground and one by one the lads came over for their share.

In the days following the pay out, I can remember standing with the 'Boss' in the car park when a few apprentices passed by. They were all suited and booted and had obviously been treating themselves following the ticket bonanza. 'I really am paying some of these lads too much,' he said, as he shook his head and with that he walked off. I was just glad he hadn't asked any questions, I was never a good liar and I'm sure I would have given the game away. Although I have no regrets, as in the end I earned much more from the tickets than I did for playing in the final itself.

Right until the last minute, the 'Boss' kept everyone (including the players) guessing about who would be playing at Wembley and then on the eve of the game he dropped something off a bombshell, by playing a formation with five across the middle which left Paul Mariner up-front on his own. A line-up of that nature is a common enough occurrence now, but was something of an innovation in those days, when four/four/two, was very much the order of the day.

Whilst the other lads were left to sweat it out, the 'Boss' had secretly told me that if I felt fit enough to play then I was in. He told me that I was still his 'Diamond' and he wanted me out there, it was a lovely gesture and definitely perked me up, although I never knew how the knee was going to be, so literally until the last minute I didn't know if I would be ok.

The knee injury became the least of my worries during an evening out with a few of the lads. It was only a couple of weeks before the final and we'd been out drinking and were making our way home in the car, when for a laugh I took off the bandage I had taken to wearing on my knee and started waving it around. It was a large compression style bandage which helped disperse the fluid which would gather around my knee and helped ease my discomfort. My good pal Robin Turner who was driving, must have been distracted by my antics because the next thing I know, we've mounted the kerb and have smashed into a lamp-post.

The car was in a real mess but miraculously we were fine, although not overly keen to hang around and wait for the police to arrive, so with the help of a good friend of mine called Bob Shelley, we soon pushed the car onto a nearby car-park and quickly got ourselves away.

There was very little that the 'Boss' missed concerning players antics and I knew the police would track us down via the number plate, so the next day, we went to see the 'Boss' and came clean. Although before we saw him, we agreed we would say things had occurred because a dog had ran into the road rather than me waving my bandage about. All went well, despite Robin messing things up and contradicting me by saying it was a cat rather than a dog which had caused the accident.

It was obviously a lame excuse and I am sure the 'Boss' had an idea of what happened, but as nobody was injured and the press hadn't been alerted, he obviously decided to let it pass and nothing more was said. It would have been typical of my luck for a silly prank to have injured both myself and other players on the eve of a big game and rob me of a lifelong ambition in taking my place in an FA Cup final and it was only afterwards that I realised how lucky we'd been.

The 'Boss' delayed announcing my inclusion in the team to the press right up until the last minute and then on the day before the game dramatic headlines about my 'surprise inclusion' appeared in the newspapers. I suppose it was a psychological ploy on behalf of the 'Boss', designed to give the fans a boost, as well as send a message out to Arsenal that we were at full-strength and meant business.

It wasn't the first time that the 'Boss' had done this, as by the side of the pitch at Portman Road was another pitch where we used to train. Every Friday, I would have my official fitness test there and the word got out amongst the fans and every week they started to come and watch and see how I was getting on. They would be shouting words of encouragement and cheering me on as I was put through my paces, which was a great feeling and definitely helped spur me on.

It was all a bit of showmanship as it was often pre-ordained as to whether I played anyway, as the quality of the opposition or the importance of the fixture saw to that. However the 'Boss' used to inject a bit of drama into it all and at the end of the session, would either give the fans the thumbs up, or down as to whether I was going to be playing or not.

Having had a lucky escape and after declaring myself fit to play, I'm not sure how the 'Boss' would have reacted when he saw me scrambling about on a police motorbike on the morning of the game. I have always loved cars and bikes and when the police escort arrived to take us to the game I couldn't resist asking them if I could have a go.

They were on the big police motorbikes reminiscent of the popular TV show of the time 'Chips' and I was soon bombing around the car-park much to the delight of the lads who were egging me on. The fun continued on the way to the game, when we were interviewed by a television crew and the interviewer mentioned that I was renowned for my strength and that I would have to be careful when shaking the hand of the Royal dignitary who on this occasion was to be Princess Alexandra.

Not really thinking I turned to the camera and said: 'Don't worry love, I won't squeeze it too hard' which amused the lads. I was a bit embarrassed afterwards, as I hadn't wanted to sound disrespectful, or for the words to come out as they did. In the end one of my team-mates came to my rescue, when David Geddis – who on the day played in midfield, overshadowed me. David, who with his blonde hair and boyish good looks was something of a heart-throb in those days, told the television interviewer he wanted to be a male model and everyone roared with laughter and immediately forgot about my gaffe.

My own comments had been remembered by one person though and as we were stood on the pitch before the national anthem, I was soon reminded of my earlier remarks. We were presented to the VIP's and eventually the Princess approached. As she went to shake my hand, she said to me 'I was watching the TV earlier, please don't squeeze too hard'. She flashed me a lovely smile and it was a terrific moment, although at the time I nearly died of embarrassment.

During the game itself, the knee held up well and I always felt in control, which made a change as I had obviously encountered so many problems in the past. I can honestly say that as a team we were never in trouble and it was the easiest game that I had played in for a long time.

The 'Boss' was of course correct in his tactical analysis and his midfield five worked the oracle and we stifled the Arsenal team as a creative force. Sammy Nelson and Pat Rice, their overlapping full-back pairing had no room to manoeuvre and big Allan and myself, hardly gave the Arsenal front two of Malcolm MacDonald and Frank Stapleton a kick all afternoon.

The only concern was that we couldn't seem to get the all

important goal. We had hit the woodwork on three occasions and I had also thundered a terrific header goal-bound only to see Pat Jennings make a brilliant save, before Roger Osborne eventually put us in front. I immediately asked the referee how long was left and we had thirteen minutes to go. Roger seemed overcome with it all and immediately after his goal had to go off as he nearly fainted.

We only had one substitute in those days and the 'Boss' sent on Mick Lambert and I overheard him telling Mick to get the ball and run it into the corner and help run the clock down. It was the right idea, although it didn't really work out, as I think Mick was so fired up and full of adrenaline. The first time he got the ball he went bombing down the wing, where he beat the full-back and promptly launched the ball into the middle of the penalty area and straight into Pat Jennings arms, who kicked the ball up-field and set Arsenal on the attack again.

We only had thirteen minutes to go, but it obviously felt a lot longer with only a one goal cushion to protect, however after an agonising wait, the whistle went and we had done it. We had won the game and I had won an FA Cup winners medal. It was obviously a terrific moment, which was made sweeter due to my prolonged injury problems.

My usual post-match routine involved rushing to the dressing room for a cigarette, although on this occasion, I didn't want to miss out on the celebrations. However I was desperate for a smoke, so I managed to cadge a cigarette from a steward and was puffing away like a steam train as I wandered around Wembley with a silly hat on my head and a blue and white scarf wrapped around my neck. It felt utterly wonderful and I was determined to soak up every minute of it all.

I was later given another surprise. We had been massive

underdogs and so I didn't realise that the bookies had priced us up at odds of 5/2. Fortunately the 'Boss' and Mick Mills were on the ball and were so sure we would win that they had taken £50 each out of our wages and lumped on. I didn't know anything about it, so when I was handed my winnings it was a nice surprise. The 'Boss' wasn't a gambling man, but he was no fool when it came to easy money either and 5/2 was a ridiculous price, although with fifty quid each riding on it, a very pleasing price all the same.

A few days after the final we had the obligatory open top bus ride around Ipswich and an official civic reception at the Town Hall. From the balcony I could see my Mum and Dad in the crowd so both Allan Hunter and myself decided to nip off and go meet them, this involved cutting through various rooms and out the back to where they were standing.

On our way out we had to pass a brass band who had been playing there as part of the celebrations. A few people wished us well and I acknowledged them and thought little else about it. The next day still feeling the worse for wear after our cup celebrations, the 'Boss' called me and Allan and told us that the police had been in touch and said that a couple of trumpets from the brass band had gone missing and that we had been seen in the vicinity. I couldn't believe it and was staggered when we were subsequently questioned by the police for several hours.

I couldn't imagine what they thought we wanted with a couple of trumpets, much less why we'd want to pinch some during celebrations for winning the FA Cup. Even if we had wanted them – which obviously we didn't, surely we had other things on our mind at the time. We were eventually allowed to go on our way, but it was an annoying incident, although I was determined that it wouldn't spoil things.

It wasn't the only shock I was to receive that day, I'd invited my Mum and Dad down for the celebrations and put them up in a local hotel and had gone over there to settle up. I peeled out a few ten pound notes from my pocket, thinking that it would cover the bill for the weekend, only to be told that it came to came to nearly five hundred pounds – this was in 1978 remember.

On closer inspection, much of the bill was for drinks, as apparently my Dad had been buying them for anyone who wanted one. In hindsight it was lucky that I'd had such a good earner out of the tickets and the £50 bet. The rest of the lads all had something to show for our unexpected little earners and started appearing in new clothes or started booking holidays. Instead of this, mine had gone on buying half of Ipswich free drinks. Although it didn't bother me too much, my attitude to money was and is, easy come, easy go.

After the FA Cup final, Robin Turner, David Geddis and myself, all Carlisle born lads who had been in the squad, were given another special day out, when we were awarded the freedom of our hometown. I am proud to come from Carlisle and I considered it a tremendous honour. Our families were there and of course everyone was very pleased for us. Apparently amongst other things, it entitles me to graze sheep on the High Street in the centre of the town. I haven't taken them up on the offer as yet, but you never know, one day I just might.

I saw the honour as a testimony to Ipswich Town's scouting policy and in particular John Carruthers. I know that a number of lads from the far reaches of the country, stretching from Newcastle across to Carlisle, ended up in Ipswich on the basis of recommendations from John and he unearthed his fair share of gems for the club.

Many years later, John was to send a talented youngster down to Ipswich for a trial. He was a chubby looking lad and didn't really look the part, although it was clear that he had great talent. Much to their subsequent regret, the club passed on the opportunity to sign him and he returned home to Newcastle. His name was Paul Gascoigne. The Boss had often labelled me, 'Daft as a brush,' a turn of phrase that he later bestowed on Paul. I suppose he rated us both as players, but realised that we both had a side to our nature where we could be a bit madcap, which often brings with it a fair share of trouble.

That side of my nature would often put me in a situation with a humorous ending, such as the time that I entered a 100 metre sprint contest to see which player was the quickest in the game. I was streets in front but within twenty yards of the winning line, my shorts began to fall down and I had to stop, in order to protect my modesty as I had no underpants on at the time. I later found out that the 'Boss' and all the lads had backed me to win, so unfortunately they lost their money.

On another occasion, whilst on an end of season tour to Bermuda, I went onto a private beach with my team-mate Eric Gates and dumped a case of lager in the sea to keep cool. After steaming into the beer, we eventually fell asleep and both got sunstroke. Eric didn't look too clever and I was even worse. I can honestly say that I have never felt as ill as I did then. I was laid in bed for two days in absolute agony and was tossing and turning about, as I couldn't get comfortable. Of course we got no sympathy from anybody and were the butt of the jokes for the rest of the tour.

My lust for life and love of a good prank often had more serious consequences though. I remember once on the way to training I was in my new car, which was a beautiful Opal Manta. We were driving down a country lane when Brian Talbot overtook me and as someone who has always been competitive and up for a challenge, I responded by speeding up and overtaking him.

I subsequently took a bend too fast and rolled the car and ended up in a ditch. I had three other players with me in the car at the time, John Wark, Robin Turner and Glen Westley. I can remember that I was laid in the car which was by now upside-down in the ditch and hearing a voice from above on the road-side saying that someone must be dead.

Eventually we all managed to scramble out of the back window – such was the state of the front end and by a miracle no one was seriously injured, although Glen had a slight cut over his eye. We were taken to a nearby naval hospital by Bobby Ferguson, who was a lovely guy and a great coach at the club. In fact Bobby was in such a panic that he probably drove there faster then we had been going in the first place.

When we arrived, the navy staff couldn't do enough for us and they were absolutely brilliant. We were given five star medical treatment and some navy rum which tasted like battery acid, although it definitely took the edge off things and the rest of the day became something of a blur. Although when the effects of the rum had worn off and I saw the state of my car a few days later, I realised how lucky we had been.

INJURY-TIME

Although the problems resulting from the crash soon subsided, the problems with my knee continued. To get me through the FA Cup final, I had received three cortisone injections, two before the game and one at half-time. On the Monday morning, once the celebrations had settled down, my knee was again swollen and painful. It was clear I couldn't go on like this and I was taken for another operation, where I had the other cartilage in my left knee removed.

I used the end of season to recuperate and returned for the start of the 1978/9 campaign however I again found that my knee was still not right. Even worse was to follow, when I damaged my other knee. It was said that the extra strain I had been placing on it may well have contributed. Although I don't suppose it mattered how it happened. All I knew was that it was giving me problems and I was eventually readmitted to hospital, where I had my third operation.

Several days later, whilst recovering at home with my leg in a plaster cast, I felt a strange sensation on my foot and I looked down and saw blood trickling down from the inside of the cast onto my toes. Obviously I had a major problem and I was immediately readmitted to hospital, where it was discovered that the stitches in my knee had been placed the wrong way around.

In layman's terms following an operation, you get two sets of stitches to help close the wound, 'proper' stitches on the outside and dissolvable ones on the inside. They had mistakenly put dissolvable stitches on the outside, so the wound left from the operation had failed to knit together. This was the reason for the bleeding, as inside the cast there was an open wound, through which you could actually see the bone.

The only solution was that I had to have another operation, which obviously meant more time on the treatment table. All I had ever wanted to do was to play football and it became an increasingly difficult and frustrating time for me. I was starting to get horribly depressed, as I had gone from being known as Bobby Robson's 'tank,' who averaged over fifty games a season to someone who struggled to play in a quarter of that amount.

I was left kicking my heels and seemed to spend all my time on the treatment table or else training on my own. I was unable to do much of anything that involved running, so I trained on my own doing weights. I would hear the lads outside having a kick about and doing things that I had once taken for granted and it was very hard to take.

I would look down at my knees and I knew that I was a long way off from getting back to full fitness. As any player who has suffered an injury will tell you, it is a very frustrating time. You feel very much on your own and you know that there is nothing much that you can do to speed up the process. You try to remain positive, although there are always nagging doubts over whether you will be the same player, or even worse whether you will play at all.

I knew at this stage, that whilst I was fighting to save my club career, my international career was over. I knew I would never recapture that pace and sharpness required to play at international level and it was very difficult to accept. I had been proud to represent my country and I had made nine under-23 and nine full appearances, however the overwhelming feeling was that it should have been more, as from the early days of my career it was always mentioned and even assumed that I would win over a hundred caps. Ironically the last game I played was against Luxembourg where I attempted to play with my injured knee. If I hadn't been so keen to represent my country and rested maybe things would have eventually been ok. Instead it was to prove to be my international swansong.

I was tipped by many to lead the England World Cup campaign to Argentina in 1978 but in the end I wasn't even in the squad due to injury. Instead I watched the games at home wondering what might have been. The amount of football that I played in was nowhere near as much as I wished, as a combination of bad luck and injury meant that I only played in around a hundred and fifty games for Ipswich Town in nearly seven seasons between 1975/81. Ironically I had managed to make the same amount in my first three seasons at the club following my debut in 1972.

I didn't know what to do with myself and I began to feel lost, as I had nothing to get up for in the morning. I needed an outlet for my frustration, so with nothing much to do I began drinking on an afternoon. I found it stopped me dwelling on my situation and helped make a long day shorter. I had always enjoyed a beer but as a footballer wasn't able to go too over the top.

After a Thursday night it was a complete no/no and I never transgressed. I prided myself on my fitness and in those days was careful about what I ate and drank. I enjoyed my share after a game on a Saturday night, especially if we had won, as it was always a great way to relax. If we had lost the game, it was also a nice way to go out and forget about things for a few hours. I was basically a typical lad, in that I saw a drink as a reward at the end of your work. Like a lot of footballers, I also enjoyed the camaraderie aspect of the game and loved knocking back a few beers with some of the lads.

At this stage, following my increasing injury problems, I found that I was beginning to drink for different reasons and because I didn't have football to focus on, I was drinking more often. I managed to make sporadic appearances on the pitch, but it was always the same problem, that after a game my knees would be horribly swollen and painful. What served to increase my frustration, was the fact that when I did make it onto the park, I was still able to perform well, albeit with the aid of cortisone.

On a Saturday, I would perform in front of tens of thousands of people and it would feel like everything was back to how it was. I would do the business on the park, receive the plaudits and generally capture the unique adrenaline rush of performing in public as a professional footballer. One epic afternoon we beat Manchester United 6-0 and amazingly both Frans Thijssen and I had missed penalties during the game.

On another occasion I lined up against the likes of the great George Best in a testimonial game for the 'Boss.' It was very strange to go from occasions like that, to hobbling around in the space of twenty-four hours. There was not only a physical transformation to deal with but a psychological one too. The cheers have subsided and the crowds have gone home and you go from that, to being left alone with your own problems and insecurities and it was something that I couldn't deal with.

I only tended to get wheeled out for the really big games, but after a time even that became difficult. It was increasingly a case of the mind being willing, but my body wasn't. One game that seemed to sum it all up was a sixth round FA Cup tie against Everton in 1980. I was again desperate to play but my injury woes only allowed me to take my place on the substitute's bench.

On the eve of the game John Wark's Dad had sadly died and he was obviously distraught. I was desperate to play, but knew that I couldn't last a full game. I know that the 'Boss' would have loved to have played me, but in the end, despite his personal situation he had to give John the nod. I came on late in the game and went up-front and within two minutes had scored. I also later hit the post and felt that if I'd been at peak fitness and on the pitch from the off, we would have won. Instead we lost the game 2-1.

I had always tried to remain positive but by the start of the 1980/81 season I began to think it was all over. Recuperation time after games now stretched to weeks rather than days and I was limited to a few substitute appearances and I knew that no football club could employ anyone in that situation. I was starting to get increasingly depressed, although I did have my mind taken off things in the most unexpected way when the 'Boss' called all the players in for a meeting one morning.

He was renowned for his meetings and they tended to drag on a bit, so his initial request inspired a moan or two. However it soon turned to intrigue, as when the 'Boss' arrived, stood alongside him was a man who introduced himself as a film producer. I couldn't work out what he wanted with the likes of us, but he went on to explain he was making a film about prisoners of war in a Nazi jail camp and he asked us if we would be interested in appearing.

It all seemed a bit grim to me and I couldn't understand how we would fit into a film of that nature. However he explained that the film had a strong football theme and that the central part of the plot, was a football game between the prisoners and the

Nazis. He said that he had already signed up other footballers such as Pele and Bobby Moore to appear and that certainly got my interest.

I was definitely sold on the idea, when he told me that the film also starred Michael Caine and Sylvester Stallone and that it was to be directed by John Huston, who was behind the camera on 'The Maltese Falcon' which starred Humphrey Bogart. The film I was asked to be involved in was of course 'Escape to Victory' and it all seemed a great way to spend a few weeks to me.

I felt that it was exactly what I needed to cheer me up and I was more than happy to offer my services. When the producer had got his volunteers, he went around the lads and began assigning people roles and eventually he got to me and he seemed to get excited and said 'Michael Caine.' I wasn't sure what he meant at first, but he explained I was to be his 'double' when they were filming the football scenes.

As soon as we arrived in Budapest, we got the full film-star treatment, as a fleet of stretch limousines were waiting for us. Although when we got to the set, we were sent straight to work. I had to go get a mask made up, which had been modelled around Michael's features and which I had to wear for the close-up shots. I also received something of a shock when I was told that I would require a hair-cut.

At the time I had my hair down to my shoulders. I'd had it that way for some years and so when the hairdresser arrived, I wasn't too keen, but it isn't every day that Hollywood calls so I went through with it. In the end the deed was done by Michael's personal hairdresser, so at least I got a top man for the job. I did get some stick from the lads though, as the previous day they'd all had their hair cut and I had been laughing at them all, little knowing that I was next up for the chop.

The main scene that I was involved in was the finale of the film, when the prisoners have the big game against the German side. It was filmed at the home ground of MTK, who are one of the lower league sides in Hungary. It was a long drawn out process, as whilst Michael is obviously a fantastic actor, he wasn't a great footballer so the days were very stop/start. A lot of the time I was left sitting around and then I would be brought on and asked to perform some kind of football action.

Then when they wanted a close-up shot of Michael they would stop filming and he would come onto the pitch and replace me. Michael was carrying a bit of weight and had no interest in the football side of things, in fact he used to make a joke of it whenever I would come on to do my thing. 'You go do my running for me, I'm off for a lie down,' he would say with a grin. He had a nice sense of humour and was always good for a bit of banter with the lads.

I got to meet Bobby Moore again, which was brilliant and he commiserated with me on my injuries, which was a nice touch, but he was a class act, so I expected nothing less. I also got to meet Pele which was a great thrill and although his English wasn't the best and my Portuguese was worse, he came across as a terrific guy. Once in between takes we started kicking a ball around and began having a contest to see who could keep the ball in the air the most times. Pele soon joined in, except that instead of a ball he used an orange. He proceeded to deliver a master-class and could do with an orange what the other lads could do a ball – it was a pleasure to watch and the man is obviously a genius.

The famous overhead kick scene he performed in the film,

was achieved on the first take. I am sure that many footballers couldn't have performed it if they'd been there all year. Although for some reason the director got him to do a few more takes, which Laurie Sivell – who was Ipswich's reserve goalie and playing the part of the German 'keeper in the film managed to save. I think that Laurie's competitive streak came out and he was determined to say that he'd saved a few shots from the great Pele.

One of the extras, who played in the German side, was in fact the Hungarian weight-lifting champion. He was a great lumbering thing and started trying to make a name for himself during one or two of the football scenes which required Michael to be a bit more involved. Basically the weight-lifter had a couple of goes at trying to nail him. Everyone saw what happened and when Michael came off and I had to go back on, he told me to go and 'do' the big man for him.

I was happy to oblige and not long into the scene my chance arrived. He was so muscle-bound and clumsy that he couldn't control the ball, which fell between us. Even with my bad knees I had the edge on him in terms of both speed and football ability, so I anticipated what was going on and turned a 50/50 tackle into one which was 70/30 in my favour. I went crunching into him in a very hard but fair tackle and as the big man really wasn't used to playing football, he went over awkwardly and hurt his back. He wasn't seen on set again, much to the delight of Mr Caine.

I found Michael to be a smashing guy, very down to earth and approachable, on the other hand I found the other star of the film Sylvester Stallone very arrogant and difficult. Unlike Michael who was happy to leave the football to the professional players, Stallone wanted to do everything himself. He was the most unlikely goal-keeper I've ever met in my life, as he's way too short for a start.

I felt sorry for my Ipswich Town team-mate Paul Cooper, who was the 'double' for Stallone and didn't enjoy the same kind of relationship as I did with Michael. 'Coops' is an easy-going fellow, who was ready to help and give advice. However Stallone seemed to think he knew it all and was very stand-offish and arrogant. I remember him always walking around with his shirt off and to be fair he had an excellent physique, apart from a huge scar down his side. I asked him what had happened and he said that he had trained so hard for the Rocky films that his skin had literally burst, an explanation which I took with a pinch of salt.

He was very much the macho-man and seemed to have had a sense of humour by-pass, so was an obvious target for a wind-up. One of the lads set to work and got him going when they told him he would never beat me in an arm wrestling contest. He took the bait and soon it was the talk of the film set and he had no choice but to take me on.

Everyone gathered around to watch the action and Stallone made it a winner take all affair for £2,000, which was obviously a lot more money to me than him. I'm not sure that by making it that amount I was meant to 'bottle' it but I was confident and things went ahead. First off we had a go left-handed and I really fancied my chances here, as basically I was a left-sided footballer and all my strength was on that side of my body.

We sat down and locked arms and there was a really brilliant atmosphere as everyone was shouting and cheering. I knew everyone wanted me to win and put him in his place and I was desperate to make sure that I won. We got the nod to start and there wasn't much resistance as I slammed his arm straight down. Everyone was singing my name and Stallone looked a bit stunned by it all.

We then commenced right-handed and although it was a more difficult proposition, I eventually beat him at that too and I claimed my money. Better still was the fact that he seemed to keep a low profile after that. Everyone congratulated me on my endeavours and after all my injury problems it provided me with a lovely boost, as well as two grand in my pocket, which was a lovely amount of money to win.

Many years later I watched one of the Rocky films with my young Grandson and I amazed him when I told him that I had once beaten 'Rocky' in an arm wrestling contest. 'No way' he replied in disbelief, 'Rocky is about seven feet tall, you could never beat him, no one could.' I conjured up a vision of the 5 ft odd Stallone I had encountered and had a little smile although I decided to say nothing. I didn't want to spoil the magic of film for a small child, as it would have been like telling him that Father Christmas didn't exist, so I kept my little secret to myself and enjoyed the memory alone.

Overall the whole journey into cinema was a fantastic experience, we were treated superbly and it gave me an opportunity to see another side of life which I wouldn't have ordinarily seen. The film has since gone on to become something of a cult classic with football fans, so it is great to have been involved with something that has stood the test of time.

After it was all over it was back to reality, as I returned to my other bit-part role at Ipswich Town. When I played, I was still able to make an impact, however it was soon apparent that it was the same old story of not being able to do it week in, week out anymore. The usual sense of frustration kicked in and I soon began to get depressed, as I no longer had the distraction of the film and was again faced with the reality that my football career was largely going nowhere.

I did make my mark, in a second round UEFA Cup game against Bohemians of Prague and people have said that I gave two outstanding performances, which were vital to the UEFA Cup run that we were enjoying at the time. We comfortably won the first leg 3-0 and looked set to go through. However upon our arrival in the Czechoslovakia, it became immediately apparent that we were also playing against the elements as the place was absolutely freezing.

I had hardly played all season, but I was happy to try and do my bit. My endeavours weren't helped by the blizzard like conditions, as there a constant downpour of sleet and snow. I really don't know how the game was allowed to go ahead and I am sure that anyone with Ipswich Town connections wished it hadn't as we soon fell behind 2-0.

It was imperative we kept them from scoring the third goal as I honestly think we would have had no chance if they had equalised. Everyone on the pitch including the Czech players had donned tights and gloves. However there was no way that I was wearing those and just like the Lokomotiv Leipzig game several years earlier, I made sure that I played – as always, wearing my short sleeved shirt. I certainly played my part and was made the man of the match, as the score remained at 2-0 and we went through on aggregate.

Although I only played eleven games during that season, it was shaping up to be a momentous season in the history of the club. As we approached the final part of the season we were fighting it out for the League Championship title and were also in the latter stages of both the FA and UEFA Cups, which of course made it an even more unbearable situation for me to be on the sidelines.

My role at this stage often involved playing in a more forward position, which was fine by me as I had started out as a striker and I proved I could still do a job when I scored in the sixth round of the FA Cup against Nottingham Forest. It was a terrific game which ended in a 3-3 draw away at the City Ground and helped keep our season going as we beat them 1-0 in the replay.

I was also fortunate to play in a more traditional position of left-full back, in a brilliant fourth round UEFA Cup tie against St Etienne, who where highly fancied to win the trophy. Not many people gave us much of a chance as we travelled to France for the first leg to face a side containing the likes of Michel Platini and Johnny Rep however they soon changed their mind after we had thumped them 4-1. A result that we followed up with another convincing victory in the second leg, as we again won easily, this time by a 3-1 margin at Portman Road. I knew we would win when I saw them line up in the tunnel and a few of their players wouldn't look me in the eye.

The great run continued and as we entered the month of April, we were still in two cup semi-finals and with a real chance of winning the Football League Championship. I was a still a peripheral figure and whilst it was devastating to know that the end of my career was nigh. I thought that winning three major trophies would be the perfect way to sign off.

The first game we faced in this historic trophy attempt, came with the first leg of the UEFA Cup which saw us line up in a midweek fixture to face FC Cologne of Germany. I was again on the bench, which I hated as I couldn't stand watching games and I was full of nervous energy as I watched an agonising game which we eventually won 1-0.

Three days later we faced Manchester City in the FA Cup semi-final at Villa Park, I started this game and I took my place in the side at left-back and was thrust into a typical semi-final game, which was tense and ninety miles an hour style football. I got the impression quite early on that it was never going to be a classic and that a goal was likely to win the game either way. I thought I had made the breakthrough and scored when I powered a text book header towards goal. I was sure that it was going in as I had made sure that I headed the ball into the ground.

Big Joe Corrigan was beaten, but after hitting the ground, the ball subsequently bounced up and over the bar. I had ironically got too good a connection. The game continued and nobody seemed able to make the breakthrough, my knees were holding up ok and I was desperate to help us get through to the final. I wanted another taste of the Wembley atmosphere, especially as I knew that I was unlikely to get this close to it again. Later in the game, I went up for an aerial challenge with City winger Dave Bennett and I comfortably beat him in the air, but in his efforts to head the ball, he instead headed my arm and I landed awkwardly and collapsed in a heap.

The physiotherapist Tommy Egglestone came on, however, when I looked at my arm and saw that it was bent out of shape, I didn't need his expert opinion to tell me what the problem was. The pain soon kicked in and my arm was quite obviously broken. I wanted to play on but wasn't allowed to. I already had two battle scarred knees and now a broken arm. It was an impossible task to carry on and unfair on the rest of the lads to have an unfit player on the park. I was led from the pitch by Tommy and was practically in tears. Not from pain but frustration, after the last few years of having constant problems with my knees, to now break my arm in such a vital game was almost too much to take. I was still determined to walk off the pitch with my head held high, although when I headed towards the tunnel, past where the Manchester City supporters were situated, they began raining down spit at me. I would usually have responded, but there was no reaction from me, as my spirit as well as my arm was broken.

Even though I was still wearing my football kit, I was immediately taken to hospital to have my arm attended to. My thoughts were still at Villa Park and I urged the medical staff to sort me out as I hoped that I might get back in time to see the finale to the game. I also kept asking for updates on the score, although nobody knew, or seemed to care, as the game was held in Birmingham and none of the locals cared who won.

I eventually returned to Villa Park, only to find out that we had gone on to lose the game by one goal to nil, with City defender Paul Power scoring from a long-range free-kick during extra-time. I got on the team bus and like the rest of the lads had a few consolation beers, although I soon wished I hadn't, as I had been given some painkillers to help with my arm and was subsequently sick on the journey home.

On arrival back at Portman Road, with my arm in a cast and feeling utterly dreadful, I was in no position to drive and so the 'Boss' drove me home. I was in a terrible state, physically and emotionally and the 'Boss' seemed to get emotional too. He gave me a hug, told me how great a player I was and what a great servant I had been to him, then because I was so shattered and Maggie was still making her way back from the game, he put me to bed. He obviously knew it was all over for me.

It signalled the end of my season, which would have been bad enough at any time, but at such a critical point in the club's history it was particularly devastating. I made a plea to be allowed to play on, but I knew that the club couldn't really entertain the idea. I thought that at one stage I would get some consolation by getting my hands on a League Championship medal, as by the last but one game of the season it was down to a two horse race between us and Aston Villa.

We had already beaten them twice that season and also knocked them out of the FA Cup in the third round, so as far as I was concerned, we were the better side. Although they had their noses in front of us and we needed them to drop points, but as their last but one game was against Arsenal at Highbury, I thought that there was every chance that we could do it.

On the same weekend, we were away at Middlesbrough, where I fancied us to get a win. It was all very tense although things looked promising when we heard that Villa had gone behind. It meant that if we won our game at Middlesbrough, then we would be entering the last game at home to Southampton, needing only a win to clinch the title. It got even better when Paul Mariner put us in front, although it was agonising for me to sit and watch this drama unfold, as I wanted to be out on the pitch. Even though I had got plenty of practice at sitting on the sidelines it was something that I never got used to.

We received news that Villa had gone further behind and the title looked likely to be on its way to Portman Road, when a previously unheralded striker called Bosco Jankovic scored twice against us, to win the game for 'Boro. Although Villa went on to also lose their game against Arsenal, they actually won the title as we needed to win both our last two games to overtake them.

I felt that both of Jankovic's goals were helped by a tired looking team, as the lads seemed to be out on their feet and I felt sure that I would have dealt with things, had I been fit enough to be on the park. I was sick at losing out and felt that an injury list containing not only myself, but also one or two other players, had left our squad looking somewhat lightweight. Essentially, the busy schedule created by our involvement in three trophies, meant that we eventually ran out of petrol at the vital moment.

I again watched from the sidelines, as we subsequently defeated FC Cologne in the second leg of the UEFA Cup semi-final to take our place against AZ67 Alkmaar of Holland in the final. I was desperate to play, not just because it was such an important game, but because I loved to play football. I begged the 'Boss' to put me on the bench, but with my arm still in a plaster cast and two weary knees supporting my body, deep down I knew he couldn't even risk me as a substitute.

The club won the trophy following a 7-2 aggregate victory, over a two-legged home and away fixture. However whilst the lads ran around the pitch waving the trophy to our fans, I felt absolutely nothing. Don't get me wrong, it was great to see the club lifting some silverware. However as any football player will verify, you don't really truly feel a part of it all unless you have contributed something on the park.

It was also an occasion tinged with great sadness, as I knew that it was the end of the road for me as an Ipswich Town player. What made it even more depressing was that my last appearance had been in the FA Cup semi-final, which had seen me leave the field with my arm broken and my shirt drenched in rival supporters spit.

I didn't want to be leaving at all and I certainly didn't want to be leaving with such a dreadful game as my swansong. It would have been nice to have obtained a UEFA Cup medal to give me a final memento, unfortunately only the eleven players on the park, plus the substitutes were awarded one, so I wasn't even given the consolation of a medal to leave with.

I had been for some time been visiting an eminent knee surgeon called Dr David Dandy who worked at Addenbroke's hospital in Cambridge, but I have to say that the visits had become increasingly demoralising as I was going nowhere in my attempt to regain full fitness. It seemed everything was tried to get me back on the pitch, but my knees would not respond. I had physiotherapy, was given exercises to do, tried rest and relaxation and as a last resort was eventually sent to a rehabilitation centre in Slough where I would arrive on a Monday morning and stay there until Friday evening.

I hated the place, as it was very spartan and there was nothing to do. I remember sitting on a machine not unlike a potter's wheel for hours on end, it was powered by a foot pump and I sat there staring into space, whilst I repeatedly pressed down my foot to get the machine going and supposedly give my knee a work out. There were no other sportsman there and it didn't appear to specialise in knee injuries, so I wondered why I was even there in the first place.

The club knew that my drinking had escalated and so I don't know if that was the reason behind sending me there, as it was a place with no distractions. However it had the opposite effect and bored me to tears and I remember climbing over the wall on an evening with some of the other patients and heading into town for a drink. Eventually I had enough altogether and checked out.

I did think that the enforced lay off due to my broken arm might do me some good, as I could rest up and hopefully that would do the trick. However the facts were simple, my knees were not getting any better and I was playing less and less games. If I did manage to play a game, the pain afterwards was unbearable. My right knee in particular would swell up to several times its normal size and I would struggle to walk to the other side of the room.

I had spent all of my adult life up to that point at the club and at only twenty-eight years old, I should still have had several good years left in me. I didn't want to leave and I wasn't sure what the future held. I couldn't contemplate life without football and all I wanted to do was get out on the pitch and play. Whenever I arrived at Dr Dandy's office, I would hope that he would tell me that he had discovered a cure, but deep down I knew he was a surgeon not a magician and every time that I arrived and nothing new happened, it was basically one step nearer to the end of the road.

The inevitable duly arrived when on one visit Dr Dandy calmly told me that I was finished as a footballer. He told me that my various surgeries, including the botched operation had damaged my knee irreparably. My right knee showed signs of arthritis and Dr Dandy spelled things out clearly and told me that I was likely to have mobility problems in later years. He also added that if I did attempt to keep playing, that I would be a virtual cripple by the time I was forty years old.

I am sure that if I had dealt with Dr Dandy from day one then things would have been different. I also don't think that the cortisone injections did me any good, but nobody forced me to have them. I could have said no, as a number of players did, so I am not pointing the finger of blame there. What is most ironic is the fact that my willingness to play and overall love of the game had contributed to my ultimate downfall.

There was nothing Dr Dandy could do for me and as he was the top surgeon in the country, there was nowhere left for me to go and so my career as a footballer was over. I have to say that it felt like I had been given a death sentence. I felt my best years were ahead of me and I had no interest in doing anything else, more importantly I could not do anything else.

I thanked Dr Dandy and went outside to my car. I closed the door and immediately burst into tears. I didn't know what to do and even though the news was not unexpected it was still impossible to take in. I went home and told Maggie and we cried together. For a time the slightest thing would trigger me off and I would burst into tears over nothing. I went to the club and obviously people were sad for me, the 'Boss' had become something of a surrogate Father to me and he was devastated.

He obviously knew it was coming and he told me he would do what he could and help get me a few quid to cushion the blow. He had a lot of contacts on Fleet Street and he helped me sell my story and several days later the headline: 'The Beat – I'm finished and it hurts like hell,' appeared as an exclusive in the News of the World. Although I remember reading the newspaper and still not believing it was for real, as if the story was about somebody else and not me.

FINAL-WHISTLE

However whilst my career was over, it was of course business as usual for everyone else. Football like time stops for no one and the club could not stop for me. They had two excellent young central defenders in Terry Butcher and Russell Osman who had come through the ranks and as the reigning UEFA Cup champions the future looked bright for everyone at Portman Road.

The club told me that they would do all they could to help me, although I was told that I might not be due a final pay-off as the insurance company claimed that my career had been ended by a degenerative injury rather than an accident. To be honest the money meant nothing to me and there was no amount on earth that I wouldn't have given to be able to continue playing football. In many ways at this stage, money was not especially an issue, I was due a testimonial and so had nice earner coming anyway. Although I can honestly say that for a long time afterwards the only thoughts I had were of still being able to play football.

With no football, I soon had nothing to do all day and plenty of time to dwell on my new circumstances, it was very difficult to take, although my spirits were briefly lifted when I went to see an Ipswich Town game against Nottingham Forest. I went to wish the lads well and whilst making my way out of the dressing room, I saw none other than Brian Clough.

'Come here' he said and so I went over to see him. With that he gave me a big hug, 'The game will miss you son,' he said tenderly. His own career had ended prematurely through injury and he commiserated with me on my predicament. 'I would have loved to have had you play in one of my teams,' he told me. His kind words meant a great deal, as not only was he a lovely man, he was also a football genius.

With the insurance row rumbling on, the club did their best and put together a committee to organise a series of events as well as a testimonial game to raise some money for me. Bob Shelley, a successful local businessman and a good friend of mine had experience of this and he was placed in charge. Bob looks like a big imposing fellow and he was nicknamed 'Maf,' as in Mafia by Mr John, with whom Bob was also good friends. Although he looks like a tough-guy, Bob is a gentle giant and as straight as an arrow business-wise, so it was good to have him on board.

He had lots of ideas and did a great job raising some cash for me, although a lot of meetings and general things concerned with the testimonial occurred at Portman Road. They weren't visits that I enjoyed, as I would see the lads training and enjoying the banter that is unique to a football club. It was unbearable and was a reminder of how my own career was over. It got to the point where I didn't want to be around the club or have anything to do with football – it was too painful.

Bob could sense how I was feeling and his reaction to it all was brilliant. He threw himself into a series of fund-raising ideas that he thought would both be a good earner and also help drag me out of my increasingly depressed state. He said that we should 'hit the road' and he set up a series of events where I was a guest speaker. Bob had organised a number of boxing promotions in the past and so he knew how to put on a show. He told me that just turning up and mumbling a few stories into a microphone wasn't enough and that we needed some glamour to pull the punters in.

We often frequented a nightclub at the time called 'The First Floor' which was a nice place where I was always treated well. The woman in charge was called Maria and was a real character who called everyone 'Baby Baby.' We had enjoyed some great nights there and one evening Bob came up with the idea of staging a Miss World style beauty pageant at the club. With the winner being given the job of adding a bit of glamour to my appearances at the various functions he had organised.

The evening went ahead and was a great success and in the end we gave three girls the job, someone christened them the 'Beat Girls' and whenever we arrived somewhere, they would be in tow. Whilst I was on the microphone, the girls would be all dolled up to the nines and be out selling my testimonial year programmes. They did a great job for me, as when faced with a nice looking girl, dazzling a winning smile at them, the punters, most of whom had already downed a bucket-full, were only too happy to oblige and the programmes would sell out every time we went somewhere.

We had some great times, I remember opening a sports shop in the town of Haverhill and it was like a Royal visit. The town was closed down and people were lining the streets. The sports shop practically sold out as people were desperate to buy something for me to sign. After the football equipment and memorabilia had gone, people were thrusting tennis racquets, boxing gloves, swimming trunks, literally anything my way for me to sign, in order to grab a memento of the day.

After the shop closed, the owner – who was obviously delighted, took us out and we had a fantastic night on the town. I returned to the hotel where we were staying, much the worse for wear and as is often the case when drunk, the practical jokes and general pranks began. Both Bob and I were looking to cause mischief, although at first we weren't sure what we could do.

We soon spotted that at the end of the corridor where our rooms were situated was a bathroom and we soon began taking it in turns running there whilst stark bollock naked. After a few goes Bob made another run for it and I decided to lock the door behind him. I left him there for about ten minutes, whilst I practically wet myself laughing. The more I laughed, the more Bob desperately asked me to let him back in. Childish stuff I know, but just what I needed to take my mind away from things.

On another evening I was due to appear at a function where we had booked the comedian Bernard Manning as the star turn. It was only before he went on stage that I noticed that a group containing the chairman's mother – Lady Blanche Cobbold were in the audience. However it was too late to issue a warning as Bernard proceeded to come on stage and from the word go he was in full blooded form.

Every other word seemed to begin with the letter F and even the most hard-faced bloke in the world would have winced at some of the gags he cracked. After the show Lady Blanche approached and I feared the worst, only for her to tell me that she hadn't laughed so much in ages and that it was one of the best nights out she had enjoyed in years.

I am sure that many people must have been envious, as to the outsider it must have looked like I was living the high life. Turning up at event after event, 'Beat Girls' in tow, signing autographs, seemingly creaming in the dough, it must have all looked good. However inside I was utterly empty, I still wanted to play football and it hadn't sunk in that it was all over. Don't get me wrong, we had some great evenings out, but it was on the wet and windy Monday mornings when it would kick in.

As well as losing my career, I had also lost the feeling of having something to look forward to. In the early days, my week was filled with training sessions, a couple of games a week and a terrific home and social life. Every week provided another challenge, another centre-forward to prove myself against, another team who were trying to beat you and stop you claiming a win bonus. It was a never ending challenge and I knew that if my form dipped, then it could see me out of the team and back working as a 'chippy' in Carlisle, so I was always motivated and driven to keep things going.

I also knew that there were literally thousands of lads who would have loved to have been doing what I was paid to do and I was always grateful for what I had and didn't want to let it go. Even when I hadn't been playing as much, there was always the hope that I might and that one day, I would wake up and things would be as they once were. Unfortunately, there was now nothing for me to do and a whole week stretching in front of me.

I would sit at home alone with my thoughts and as I began to dwell on things I would be overcome with depression. It is a difficult feeling to explain to someone who hasn't been through it. I wanted no sympathy and expected no sympathy as I knew from my own experiences back home in Carlisle that there were a lot of people worse off than me. However there was a huge void in my life and nothing to fill it.

Rather than sit at home moping, I would head out for a drink. There was always someone to talk to and a long, boring day was made much shorter. I have always been a sociable person and being out and about seemed a natural way to solve my problem.

At first you can't see any harm in it all and a few drinks seemed to take the edge off things and help me sleep better on an evening. I suppose I subscribed to the theory that Frank Sinatra put forward when he once famously said: 'I feel sorry for people who don't drink, as when they wake up, that's as good as they feel all day.' Although of course after a while you don't feel good at all, you feel terrible. That's how it was for me, my mind was all over the place and I had a lot of pent up energy and as I have never been the most organised person, there were times I wasn't always where I should have been. One evening I had been booked to do a question and answer session at a small town called Diss and I had completely forgotten about it and had gone away to Malta for a few days.

I hadn't meant to let people down and it also meant that Bob Shelley was left out on a limb, as the punters were already there waiting. He had to get on stage and say that I was running late as my car had broken down. Obviously the reality as to what had really happened had got out as when Bob made his statement, someone in the crowd shouted back at him: 'Where's his car broken down – Valletta? I felt dreadful when I heard what had happened, although it was a clear sign that my mind was pre-occupied and my thoughts were taken up as much with my football past, as they were with my future.

I eventually had something to occupy my time when I eventually had my testimonial game in 1982, where my opponents were Dynamo Moscow. It was obviously an evening of differing emotions for me. On the plus side, it provided me with the opportunity to properly say my goodbyes to the fans and also bow out in a more dignified manner than I had in the FA Cup semi-final.

On the downside it also signalled the end of an era for me, as a twelve year association with Ipswich Town would be over. In the run up to the game, I was of course the subject of a fair bit of press and TV coverage and I was always asked the same questions about how I felt and what I was going to do next. I seemed to say the right things and keep them all happy, but inside I didn't have a clue and it was almost like I was talking about someone else and not me.

The Dynamo Moscow side were accompanied on the trip by several KGB representatives, who I believe were there in case any of the players enjoyed life in England a little too much and didn't want to return home. They were also accompanied by football legend Lev Yashin, who had a friendly demeanour and as always, it was a thrill for me to get to meet a football great. He was a big guy and had hands like a couple of coal shovels. I never thought I would live to see someone with bigger hands than my Dad, but Lev beat him, well hands down.

He seemed to have one of them permanently wrapped around a glass of whisky and whilst he couldn't speak English he seemed to speak the same language as Mr John. The last I saw of Lev, he was in his office roaring with laughter at Mr John's antics, as the pair of them polished off a bottle of best Scotch between them. As it was definitely going to be my last game for the club, I have to say that I felt like joining them.

The game itself was a typical testimonial and more about the occasion rather than any football. Despite the injury, I made sure that I was on the park, but with the knee troubling me, I came off near the end. I received a standing ovation from the crowd and stood in the middle of the pitch with my arms in the air as I applauded all sides of the ground. I then made my way from the pitch, as I felt the tears welling in my eyes. I looked at the 'Boss' and I could see that he was emotional too. I really didn't know what to do at this point. All that I knew was that my life was going to be very different from this moment on and I really didn't know what to make of it all.

I had an attitude that something new would turn up tomorrow, although when tomorrow eventually arrived nothing was happening. Bob Shelley could see what was going on and did his best to help and he talked to me about making a playing comeback as it would give me something to focus upon. It was clutching at straws, but for a time it did give me something different to get up for in the morning.

Bob was a decent amateur boxer and was always out training and he said we should start working out together and that he would act as an unofficial agent for me and get in touch with a few clubs. I had for the last few years only made sporadic appearances at Ipswich and I figured I could probably manage to do that somewhere else. Although I wasn't sure that somebody would want me under those circumstances. However, I figured that I had nothing to lose and if I could even prolong my career by another season or two then it had to be better than sitting around at home doing nothing.

Although deep down I knew that my knees were never going to be right and it was hard to train not only from a physical point of view, but a psychological one too. I knew I could manage a game here and there and for all the pain that resulted, it hardly seemed worth it. However I decided it was better than drinking myself into oblivion and I got stuck into the training.

I had to avoid any running and instead pounded the weights and worked on my upper body strength. I was a naturally fit person

At Portman Road – the kipper tie has gone but the passion for the club remains.

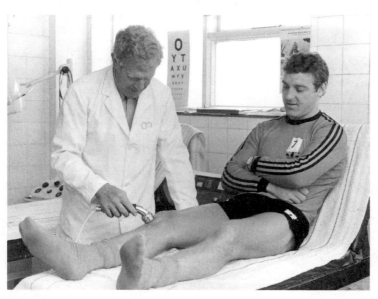

A familiar sight as I get treatment on my knees. I look reasonably carefree but inside I was becoming a troubled soul.

My appearances on the park became a rarity, so our 1978 FA Cup
win felt so wonderful.

Parading the FA Cup to the fans at our civic reception – the bottles
of bubbly had obviously been flowing.

The FA Cup also provided me with one of the worst moments of my career, as I break my arm against Manchester City in the semi-final in 1981. It was to be my last game in an Ipswich Town shirt.

On the comeback trail with my good friend Bob Shelley.

Another fantastic footballer who had his troubles away
from the game – with the great George Best.

(left)
I finally get my hands on the UEFA Cup – yet another injury had denied me my chance of glory in 1981.

(below)
I'm presented with a replica of my 1974 PFA Young Player of the Year award by Ipswich Town Chairman David Sheepshanks. I lost the original in a fire.

anyway and after a few weeks, I was soon ready to give it another go. Bob knew the Norwich City manager at the time Ken Brown and I soon began training with them and although I was in some discomfort, the knee seemed to be ok. Ken had always rated me and offered me a short-term contract.

It seemed strange to be about to sign for 'The Canaries,' as of course I was still very much associated as being an Ipswich Town player. However I liked Ken and as there were some decent lads at the club, I shook hands on a deal and went home. The next day I received a call from Ken, who said that the deal was off. I was upset and couldn't understand why, however he told me that Ipswich still held my registration as a player and were reluctant to let me go to their big rivals.

There were also still unresolved issues regarding my insurance pay-out. I told Ken that I wouldn't play against Ipswich and was happy to have that inserted into my contract. To be honest, I would have found it difficult to have lined up against them anyway and so a clause of that nature seemed the perfect solution. However it was all to no avail and I was not allowed to sign.

Whilst this occurred I received an offer to go and play for Colchester United, my old team-mate Allan Hunter had taken over as player-manager there and had inherited a young and in-experienced squad. He asked if I fancied signing for them as I would add a bit of experience about the place. I didn't need asking twice and so I signed immediately.

I played for Allan for a few games and things went ok and it was nice to be involved again. Although I soon realised that I could never be the same player that I once had been and I would descend into bouts of depression whilst I was at home on my own. I had begun playing with a knee support on my right knee which was particularly troublesome and it served as a constant reminder. When I played I pulled my socks up high to try and cover it up but I wasn't fooling anyone, least of all myself.

I soon realised that I wasn't the only person with problems when after a few weeks at Colchester tragedy struck. One of my new team-mates John Lyons suddenly committed suicide. Everyone at the club was devastated, although nobody could understand why it had happened, as he was a lovely lad, who seemingly had everything going for him.

There was a very sombre atmosphere around the club and I think it all eventually proved too much for Allan in having to deal with such a horrible situation as that. He was still learning the management ropes and he eventually quit. It made me assess my own position and whilst I worked out what I was going to do next, I got the opportunity to go and sign for Middlesbrough.

The move came about through Bob Shelley, who felt that I should have one last crack with a big club. The manager at the time was one of the great characters in football – Malcolm Allison, which was a big attraction for me, although I guess with my situation, there wasn't a lot of options open to me. I didn't know how long it would last and I signed for the club on the basis that we all knew that my knees were in poor condition and that it could all be over at any time.

I wasn't going to up sticks and move to Middlesbrough permanently on that basis and so after signing for the club, I ended up staying in the same hotel as Malcolm and his family. Bob also accompanied me and it was good to have him around. Malcolm was also good company and he didn't believe in doing things by half and he enjoyed life to the full. We'd eat at the hotel, get our laundry done, in fact everything was only a room-service call away.

I got on very well with Malcolm and we would often sit in the hotel late into the night enjoying a few drinks and he became more of a friend than my manager. He left much of the day to day stuff to his assistants Cyril Knowles and George 'Geordie' Armstrong, who were also good guys. In fact to be honest the only real contact I had with Malcolm was after the game when the champagne started flowing.

Once before a game away at Chelsea, Malcolm kindly allowed me to travel to the game on my own. He loaned me his Jaguar for a few days, so I went down to Ipswich and spent a couple of days there and then made my way to Stamford Bridge – arriving there around 2.00pm. It was no real surprise to not see Malcolm there and to find Cyril and Geordie in charge, however even they started to get a bit anxious when by 2.30pm Malcolm still hadn't arrived.

Eventually at ten to three, Malcolm burst into the dressing room with a shopping bag from Harrods in his hand. Someone asked him where he'd been and from the bag he pulled out a brand new fedora hat, which was of course his trademark. He put it on his head and then he lit up a cigar, which was the size of a stick of Blackpool rock. A huge grin spread across his face as he turned around to his inquisitor and said : 'It's pissing down out there son and I wouldn't want to get my cigar wet would I?' With that he walked off roaring with laughter. That was Malcolm – a complete one off and life was very different under him in comparison to what I had known at Ipswich.

I remember that Malcolm once asked me who I thought should be playing in the team. I wasn't used to a manager asking me my opinion in this way and at Ipswich I would have been astounded if the 'Boss' had asked me such a thing. I'm not saying Malcolm was wrong it was just not what I was used to. I did find Malcolm to be an outstanding coach though – as he had obviously proved in the past, especially at Manchester City.

He had a lot of ideas on the game and was a very interesting guy to talk to. He had been an excellent player himself at West Ham, until a bout of tuberculosis finished his career. Ironically Malcolm's replacement was none other than Bobby Moore, the man who I was tipped to replace at one stage. Malcolm was a shrewd man and appreciated that football players have a short attention span and so made sure that the atmosphere, especially in training was always bright and breezy.

He would get us to try other things to help improve our sharpness and keep our interest. On one occasion, he brought in a guy called Len Hepple, who was the ex-Sunderland and Newcastle striker Bryan 'Pop' Robson's father in law, to teach us ballet. Even though none of us could do any of the moves that Len was trying to teach us, it at least got everyone bonding together. Even if it was just to laugh at each other as we made total fools of ourselves. One of my best pals at the club was the striker Ray Hankin who I loved to bits. Ray was definitely built for comfort not speed and watching him attempt to perform the ballet moves was one of the most surreal and funny things that I have ever seen.

Whilst living in the hotel with Malcolm, I was thrilled to meet the band Whitesnake when they rolled into town for a gig. They were staying in the same place as us for a few nights and turned out to be a great bunch of lads. I've always been a rocker at heart and I got on famously with them – in particular the drummer Cozy Powell. I saw them at their show in town and they were terrific and when they invited me to the next gig on their tour I didn't need asking twice.

It was straight after the game on a Saturday night and I shot down to Manchester for the gig and in the VIP bar before the show, the first person I saw was Alex 'Hurricane' Higgins, who I had met many times before as he often came to Ipswich to play snooker. I knew Alex enjoyed a good time and the Whitesnake boys weren't exactly shy either, so I knew it would be an eventful evening.

After the show – which was brilliant, we headed across town to Alex's house which he'd bought from George Best. It was a very famous place, not only due to the fact that George had once owned it when he was at the height of his fame, but also due to its futuristic design. It was a really strange shape and almost exclusively made of glass rather than bricks.

We went down into the cellar, where Alex had a snooker table and it was on this occasion that I tried drugs for the one and only time in my life. I tried a few lines of cocaine, although I couldn't even get one line up, as my nose had been broken so many times. We started to have a game of snooker, when all of a sudden the cocaine must have kicked in. I felt terrible and knew that I had to get back to the hotel.

I remember waking up the next day in the bath, I had been sick everywhere and felt terrible. Up until the drugs incident, I had enjoyed the night and I vowed never to get involved in the drugs scene again. I tried it once and it wasn't for me and my advice to anyone is to stay clear. After spending all of the following day in bed, I eventually had to make a move back to Middlesbrough to be back at training on the Monday morning.

On arrival I wasn't feeling much better, so I went straight to see Malcolm and told him I couldn't train and came clean as to why, telling him all about the cocaine. I expected a bollocking, if not being shown the door, but instead Malcolm replied: 'Don't worry son, we've all being there' and he left it at that. Looking back, I think I only did the 'coke' as I needed some kind of excitement, as I knew the buzz that I had always got from football was over. It was hard to enjoy playing when in the back of your mind you know that every game could be your last.

In the end I only managed a few games for Malcolm, when my injury woes struck again, although ironically it wasn't my knee which signalled the end of my spell in the North East. It came in the midst of a terrific game which I was really enjoying against Newcastle United. It was a cracking derby atmosphere and a really tight competitive game of football, I was marking Kevin Keegan and getting a buzz from pitting my wits against a top player as he undoubtedly was.

I was chasing after a loose ball, when I stretched to put in a clearance and ripped a muscle in my groin. I knew it was serious as soon as I had done it, as I actually heard a noise as if someone had unzipped a sleeping-bag. I was eventually carried away on a stretcher from the game and I was told that I would be out for several months. One of my knees was also playing up again and I now knew that I had definitely hit the end of the road as a professional player.

I was of no use to Malcolm anymore, so I said my goodbyes and left. In the few games I played, I managed to turn in good performances, so I had proved my worth to the club, but the fact was that I couldn't do it anymore. It had been great fun to work with Malcolm, who was a great coach and a lovely guy. He had an incredible sense of fun and had treated me really well. Malcolm was under pressure himself, as the club had run out of money and not long after my own departure, he also left the club. His replacement after a brief spell as caretaker manager by Jack Charlton, was Willie Maddren, the man who the 'Boss' had tried to sign for Ipswich Town all those years ago.

I had to accept that I could never play football to the standard I had managed before and that the days of playing for a top flight side were over, although it was easier said than done. Around the same time I eventually came to an agreement on a pay-out from Ipswich Town regarding the fact that my career was now definitely over, which was not good news in some ways as the money was soon burning a hole in my pocket.

I admit I have never been good at handling money, as far as I am concerned it is there to be spent and enjoyed and if I can put a smile on other people's faces by throwing a few quid about then so much the better. I again sought solace in the pub, there was always company to be had and it would take me away from my problems. It also made me feel good about myself if I could buy someone a drink and help them forget their own worries. Of course there were no shortage of takers and looking back my generosity was seen as a weakness and I was taken advantage of.

My situation wasn't helped when my Dad passed away. Years of hard drinking had finally caught up with him and he died a relatively young man of 52. We were never as close as I would have liked and after I moved to Ipswich, I only saw him on a few occasions. He actually only ever came to see me twice, once for my wedding and on another occasion when he arrived unannounced to see a game.

He was a typical hard-drinking Northerner and he wasn't the best at expressing his feelings, but he was my Dad and I know that in his own way, he was proud of the fact that I had played for a top football team, as well as my country. It was a terrible moment when I heard the news that he had gone, although the manner of his passing should have provided a cautionary tale for me. However, it only served to want to make me drink more as I now had something else to feel bad about.

I had received a reasonable pay-out and had obviously been used to a decent standard of living whilst at Ipswich Town. However I was now not earning any wages, but probably spending more than ever. I had never saved any money and I knew I couldn't keep spending without earning. I couldn't do anything else and still couldn't see a life beyond football, so I ended up playing few games for Barnet under their then manager Barry Fry.

If I thought big Mal at Middlesbrough was a character, then Barry Fry left him standing. Barry was a laugh a minute and he certainly engineered a great team-spirit at the club. He knew the score regarding my knee and I basically turned up for games and wasn't required to do any training. In return Barry knew that even at 50% fit I was still head and shoulders above anyone playing at that level of football.

He also knew that as well as providing a bit of extra experience and class on the park, as an ex-England international, I might also help drag a few extra punters through the door and help pay my way. Barry had also struck a similar deal with another ex-England international in Steve Whitworth, so for a brief time, non-league Barnet were able to field a back four containing two ex-England footballers.

Barnet's home ground Underhill, was a pretty notorious place. It was more like a park pitch than the home to semi-professional team, which they were at the time. It wasn't even flat and it had a huge slope and the terrible drainage meant that it often ended up resembling a paddy field. Barnet used it to their advantage, which was fair enough, although it wasn't doing my knees any good and it wasn't long before my old problems soon resurfaced.

I have to admit that my drinking was escalating at this time and I wasn't the world's most reliable person. I actually missed one game by failing to turn up, much to the displeasure of Barnet chairman Stan Flashman, who of course I knew well following the FA Cup ticket bonanza a few years earlier. Stan could be very generous, but I knew he was also a man not to trifle with however a combination of the drink and depression makes you very self-absorbed and less than bothered about what's happening elsewhere.

I only found out years later that Stan had got a message to people close to me, telling them that if I ever failed to turn up to another game, he would make sure I no longer had knee trouble, as he would have them both blown off with a shotgun. Whether he would have is anyone's guess, although fortunately he never got the chance, as because of my injuries I told Barry that I couldn't do a job for him anymore and I quit.

I never saw Stan again, but I parted on good terms with everyone else – especially with Barry. He has a lust for life and is a wonderfully charismatic person, who I still stay in touch with. I have done a bit of coaching for him at Peterborough and he remains as ever, one of the great characters in the game.

After I left Barnet, things went drastically downhill. I still had money left over from my pay-off, but nothing else coming in. I applied for a few coaching jobs but no one was interested, I had been a professional footballer since I was sixteen years of age, so I was qualified to do nothing else and getting other types of work also proved difficult. As a result most of my days were spent in the pub. I was living in a haze and unable to deal with the reality of my situation. Day after day, month after month, I was on the same treadmill and the pub was always a wonderful escape as there was always another lost soul to prop up the bar with and it was the only place where my problems would vanish.

I was moving in fairly desperate circles and everyone seemed to be drinking to escape some sort of problem. There seemed to be this unwritten code of conduct where nobody would ever confront you with a version of reality and you would sink into oblivion together. Of course it cannot go on, as everyday you wake up and nothing has changed, except that in my case one thing had, as my money was slowly but surely running out.

My financial difficulties were such, that I was soon unable to meet the bills as they arrived on the doormat. I needed some quick money, so I was forced to sell my house and sold it for a lot less than it was worth, so in the long run I essentially lost money on that particular deal. It kept the creditors at bay for a while and we were eventually re-housed by the council. Of course that money eventually runs out as well and you are back to square one and the whole mess seems to be a never-ending state of affairs.

Things came to a head, when I eventually fell behind with my rates bill to the council. Eventually the debt was passed on to a collection agency and the bailiffs started arriving. It was a horrible time, as you feel like a prisoner in your own home, every knock on the door fills you with dread and you feel there is nowhere for you to turn. Most people are granted anonymity in this situation however my predicament soon became public knowledge as the newspapers got wind of things.

There was one occasion when there were actually two groups of people outside on the doorstep chasing me, one made up of bailiffs and the other who were journalists. The bailiffs used the situation to their advantage, as they knew they had an opportunity to keep going public and shame me into paying them the money. However the reason I hadn't paid up, was because I didn't have it and so I couldn't give them what I didn't have. I found myself in a horrible vicious circle, whereby all my problems had me increasingly reaching for a drink, when the only solution was going to arrive if I could stay sober and find decent work.

In the end, with no work forthcoming and my drinking escalating by the day, I had no other option and I came to an arrangement whereby the bailiffs took my FA Cup winners medal as security on the debt. It was heartbreaking, but it was the only asset I had left and it was subsequently sold to a local businessman and I used the money to wipe the slate clean.

It is at times like this that you begin to realise who your friends are, as many of the people that I had been spending time with suddenly disappeared. It's a situation you have heard of a million times before, but it doesn't make it any easier when it happens to you. I found that a lot of people had been hanging around with me because I had been a professional footballer, or because I had a few quid in my pocket, not because they actually liked or respected me.

I was renowned as a big-hearted person on the pitch and I suppose I was big-hearted in the pub as well. When the money finally went, I wasn't looking for sympathy, or a hand-out which is just as well, as the general consensus from people was one of: 'You have had money and blown it, so why should we help you out?'

There have been one or two exceptions, I remember a guy I knew called Phil Mann who was a big Ipswich Town fan and he gave me a car to run about in. When I went to collect it, he told me there was something inside the dashboard for me. When I opened it there was an envelope with £500 inside. When I told Phil that I would pay him back, he told not to bother and that it was 'payment' for all the good memories that I had provided him with over the years.

Bob Shelley has always been a good friend and he has helped me out both financially and emotionally. He is a very generous man, who has a lovely home in Ipswich and I would regularly pop over there to see him. At one stage, he had an eccentric one-armed gardener called Percy, who spoke with a lisp. He was always good for a laugh and after a visit to see him and Bob I would always feel better afterwards.

Another local businessman called Ian May has also been a great friend. He was an unofficial agent for me and tried to help me get back on my feet and although things didn't really work out, I appreciate all of the things that he has done for me. Another good friend who I can depend on is Duncan Foster – he has helped me out with a few quid here and there when I have been short and is someone who is always there for me.

Latterly, a terrific pal has been a journalist called Dave Allard. He was for many years, the man who covered all the Ipswich Town games, so he was always around at Portman Road and I have known him a long time professionally. In the last few years we have also become good friends. He has helped me in so many ways and has been a terrific person to have around and is a guy whose company I appreciate tremendously.

However in the past, good friends have often been few and far between and with the debts still mounting and my prized medal gone, I knew I had to do something. I tried to get my act together and eventually found work as a labourer on a building site. I am not knocking anyone who does it, but it was hard to take when I was still only thirty years old and entering what would have been my prime as a footballer and I have to say that it was a cold and lonely place to be.

It was impossible to deal with the reality of it all, especially when I used to watch the football on the television and think that I should still be playing. Instead I was up to my ears in filth, working for peanuts. It was hard work and I would arrive home exhausted. The wages were poor and it seemed that I was no better off than before although I kept going as I knew that I had no alternative.

Eventually the newspapers picked up on what I was doing and there seemed to be a few jibes about how I now earned my living. It seemed that whatever I did, it not only failed to improve my situation, but it also ended up in the press, where I was made out to be some kind of 'fallen hero.' I remained in constant financial difficulty and every time something happened, the stories of my various woes always seemed to make the press. I seemed to be making the newspapers as often as I did when I was playing although now my problems were making the front pages rather than the back.

They have a job to do and as someone who was in the public eye, I accept that they will always be interested in whatever I do. I also accept that the nature of the press will always make them interested in stories where someone is encountering problems. Though I accept the state of affairs, it is still a very difficult situation to take, especially when you are the person on the receiving end of it all.

I was spending a lot of time in a pub called 'The Drunken

Docker,' which was probably as rough as it sounds. In actuality it was two barges welded together which was moored on the River Orwell in Ipswich. I had spent a fortune in there over the years and when the money was running out, I cashed a cheque with the landlord for £100. However I didn't know that I hadn't enough funds in the bank to cover the money and it subsequently bounced.

Rather than try and sort something out with me, the people who owned the pub went to the newspapers and told them about the story and also had my cheque framed and put over the bar. It was manna from heaven for the press and made for a great article for them as headlines such as: 'Ex-star Beattie in cheque disgrace' and 'The disgrace of a former Town and England idol,' appeared in the newspapers.

As well as been constantly referred to as a 'fallen hero,' there also seemed to be a reference to how much money I had made from my pay-off. I had actually made around £30,000 which is obviously a lot of money. Although I did hear that another ex-England player who finished at the same time as me due to a similar injury left the game with nearer to a quarter of a million pounds.

Much of the money I made was sent back to help my family out in Carlisle, more was spent in the hostelries of Ipswich. I was also too generous and some may even say naive. I was seeing life through a haze of depression and alcohol at this time so I wasn't aware of what I was doing. However I have heard stories that I have given strangers considerable sums of money and also handed over personal football memorabilia that would now be worth thousands of pounds to people I hardly knew for nothing.

At the time it felt good to be making other people happy, you are the life and soul of the party and everyone is pleased to see you and it feels better than sitting at home feeling miserable. Although of course the party can't last forever and when any party is over and all the guests have gone home, all you are left with is a lot of mess to clean up, which is exactly how it was for me.

You don't realise what has happened at first, you get used to a certain standard of living and a way of life and it's only a slow realisation that things have changed. I wished I had more to show for the money, I am especially regretful that Maggie and my three lovely girls also suffered. However if I frittered it away then so be it. It might make me misguided, naive or even foolish however I don't see how it would necessarily make me a bad person or indeed a 'fallen hero.' As far as I could see, all I had done was spend my own money.

It was now only two years since I had been part of an Ipswich Town side which had come agonisingly close to winning the triple whammy of the Football League, FA Cup and the UEFA Cup and my downhill journey had been rapid and I was nearing rock bottom. I had tried to get a variety of coaching jobs, but I think the football grapevine was aware of my drinking and no professional teams would touch me.

So in order to supplement my wages from the building site, I began playing on park pitches and local recreation grounds for a local team called Harwich and Parkeston. The money from the pay-off had gone and I was reliant on the money they paid me to help make ends meet. My match fee was twenty pounds a game. After the game there was always a raffle to raise a few quid for club funds and the manager – a great guy called Tony Armstrong, always made sure that I won a joint of meat or something to eat, so as to help keep things going for a few days.

Obviously the other lads knew what was going on, but nothing was said. I felt embarrassed that it had got to this and it became something of a standing joke when every week a ticket bearing my name would be pulled out. The lads didn't mind though and were just happy to have me on board, as many of them were Ipswich Town fans and were amazed to be lining up alongside me, having previously watched me from the terraces.

I have to admit that I was finding life on the building site increasingly difficult, not only was it hard work, but I am easily bored and I soon get restless. I admit that I am not good at keeping myself organised, or getting up early and I find it hard to stick at things. I was desperate for an opportunity to do something else, although I couldn't see a way out and it seemed a battle just to get through each day. Then whilst I was wondering where I would go next, I received an offer from Ron Gray, the man who had originally met me on my first visit to Ipswich.

Ron had established some contacts in Scandinavia and managed to find me a club in Sweden called Sandvikens, who played in the Swedish second division. The standard wasn't great but the financial package was ok – albeit only a hundred pounds a week. The main attraction was that I had genuinely had enough of life in England and was in desperate need of a fresh start. With that in mind, I literally snapped Ron's hand off and accepted his offer on the spot.

I found Sweden to be lovely clean country and its people were extremely courteous and friendly. I was grateful of a new beginning and it was a wonderful place to bring up the kids for a while. As the money from the football wasn't enough to live on, it was a pre-requisite of getting a visa that you had another job and I began working for a sports kit supplier to supplement my wages and I gradually got back on my feet.

The standard of football wasn't great, but it was nice to be playing regularly and the regime of constant training and playing kept me away from the booze, which also felt good. I began playing up-front and was soon knocking in the goals and the manager of the team was pleased with me. He was a really decent guy and we got on well. His name was Thomas Nordahl and he had been an excellent player in his own right, who had been in the Swedish squad for the 1970 World Cup. His father Gunnar had played for AC Milan and he must have been some player, as he actually still holds the record for the most goals scored in a single Serie A season, scoring 35 in 1949/50.

Even though my knees would never be right, the standard of football was so far behind what I had been used to, that I didn't have to put in anywhere like the effort I would in England. As a result I managed to play without any great reaction afterwards. After a lovely season, where I became the club's player of the season, I felt good about things again, unfortunately Thomas quit as the manager of the club and the new manager didn't want me, as I think he saw me as a threat to his job, so the club let me go.

Luckily I was soon offered a contract by a club in Norway called Kongsberg. Once again the wages weren't up to much and neither was the standard of football – the Norwegian fourth division. However even with bad knees it was easy. Just as I had in Sweden, I needed another job to supplement my wages and fortunately a guy called Tjell Hauge, who was connected to the club, was a big English football fan and so knew who I was.

We went for a drink and he told me that he was the manager of a hotel and that he would give me a job as the manager of the hotel bar. It probably wasn't the wisest of decisions given my track record with the booze however I needed a job, not only for the money, but also to get the visa, so I wasn't in any great position to say no.

Norway proved to be very similar to life in Sweden and the football was again very easy for me. I continued to play as a striker and even with my knee problems I was able to score over sixty goals in my first season with the club. There were some decent lads there and I was treated as something of a star as I had played in the top-flight in England which is very popular in Scandinavia. It was also a lovely place to bring up my children, as it was so safe and clean and the process of getting back on my feet continued.

Whilst I wasn't earning much money, or playing to the standard I wished, I tried to be philosophical about it all and enjoy what I had rather than what I didn't have. I did my best to make a go of it all and I went through all the necessary training on how to run a bar, which kept me busy for a time. Although in the end my job in the hotel was relatively quiet, as the exorbitant prices of alcohol prevented people from drinking too much. Even back then, a pint cost four or five pounds a time and the average person couldn't afford too many nights out at those prices. I think that's why I initially got the job, as I might have given someone the added incentive of popping in for a drink.

The locals loved their football and a lot of them couldn't quite believe that a top footballer from England was now working behind the bar of their local hotel and so whilst we weren't overrun with trade, there were always one or two curious people who called in to see me for a drink and a chat. Although most people had to be selective about when they came for a drink in the hotel, they weren't exactly going without. I eventually found out that most of the locals used to make something called 'hjemmebrent' which translates to 'home burnt.' It was basically moonshine, which was made from potatoes, sugar, yeast and water.

It was actually illegal, but nobody seemed to mind. I remember once going into the local supermarket and whilst I was in the queue to pay for my goods, I noticed that everyone else who was also queuing up had a trolley which contained several kilograms of sugar and bags of potatoes. It didn't take a genius to work out why.

To be honest everyone was at it, even a neighbour of mine at the time who was the local police chief. He was a big football fan and we got on well and he soon invited me over to his house and asked me if I fancied a drink. I was expecting an ice cold can of lager, but instead out came the 'hjemmebrent.' He had added essence of vodka to flavour it up and he loved it, but to me it was more like paint-stripper.

He once took me and a group of others on a fishing trip onto one of the nearby fjords. It was a beautiful, sunny day and was one of those days when everyone is having a good time. It was one of the best days out that I had enjoyed for some time, although following the appearance of a few bottles of 'hjemmebrent' to help while away the hours, the only thing that we managed to catch was a stinking headache apiece.

The Norwegian people were very sociable and I would have been happy to have remained over there permanently. However I wasn't earning enough to cope with the incredibly high cost of living. Allied to that was the fact that Maggie was getting homesick and she was concerned about bringing up the kids in a country where English wasn't the first language.

We put a few feelers out and Maggie's sister sent us a cutting for an advertisement for a couple to live in a pub and run it on a management basis back in Suffolk. I had obviously acquired the necessary skills working with Tjell and so I applied. I got the job and we made plans to come back home to England. I had stayed three seasons in Norway and towards the end of my stay had signed for second division team called Nybergsund, where I also performed well. I thoroughly enjoyed my time in Scandinavia and it certainly helped me get some self-respect back and whilst I was sorry to be leaving I didn't feel that I had much alternative.

It's at times like this, that you are looking around for good friends and I found two in Duncan Foster and Faz Madini. Both of these guys are fanatical Ipswich Town fans and when they heard I was coming back to the UK, they were very helpful to me. I was struggling financially as the high cost of living had become a drain on my wage packet. Both Faz and Duncan were there when I needed them and for that I will always be grateful. Faz's lovely wife Sharon was also a good friend to Maggie which I am also thankful for.

My impending move to the UK filled me with some trepidation, as I had a lot of bad memories associated with the last period of time I had spent there. Drinking my life away and struggling to make ends meet was not what I wanted a return to. Although I tried to look at the new pub management job as a fresh chapter in my life. As much as I had enjoyed Scandinavia and as proud as I am to come from Carlisle, Ipswich was in many ways still my spiritual home. It's a place that I have a huge amount of affection for and I felt that it was the best place to head to, as I went on my journey of personal rehabilitation and continued the quest to bring some meaning into my life following the loss of my professional football career. Though little did I know what life had in store for me.

POST-MATCH

Whilst we were in the process of sorting things out, I came back to the UK for a social visit and was immediately arrested at Harwich sea port. I hadn't a clue what for and was subsequently taken to the police station and charged with failing to pay an outstanding fine for two overdue library books. Apparently before we had left for our new life overseas some three years previously, Maggie had forgotten to take back two library books she had borrowed.

The library service had been sending reminders to our old address in Ipswich and obviously as we had moved abroad we never had the chance to respond. The books had been borrowed on a ticket that was in my name and it had been requested that I be prosecuted. I explained why we hadn't been in touch and it all seemed very heavy-handed to me, I offered to settle the debt, but they didn't want to know and I was eventually taken to court.

It was waste of public money and I wondered if I hadn't been an ex-footballer whether I would have suffered the same fate. I was fined £25 and ordered to pay £10 in court costs. It made the newspapers and the whole charade was used as another chapter in the story of my 'fall from grace.' After it was all over, I did have a wry chuckle when I discovered one of the titles of the books in question, it was called 'Indifferent Heroes' by Mary Hocking.

As if this scenario wasn't enough, whilst I was in the process of moving back home, I had put most of my gear in storage with a friend over in Norway who had a large farm. He kept my belongings in his barn which unfortunately one evening caught fire and I lost all of my possessions. Some of it was replaceable, but amongst the lost items were what was left of my trophies, caps and football memorabilia.

We had no insurance to claim on and the football items were irreplaceable anyway, as no amount of money could have made up for losing them. I was devastated and it really did seem like it was one thing after another. The worst part was that there was nothing I could do except try and forget about it and it made the move back to the UK even more important.

When I arrived, I decided that I would throw myself into my new pub management job and try and forget about things, it was good to be home and the word was soon out that I was back in town. This was good news, as it meant that we were getting plenty of punters through the door. We worked hard to build up the customer base and as there were plenty of Ipswich Town supporters around, we soon had a nice busy pub, which turned over decent business.

Maggie was a florist by trade and so kept the place looking nice with fresh flowers. As mine host, I was there to help generate a positive vibe and as everyone was pleased to see me, it was an easy enough task. For a while, everything was going really well, it was great to be back in Suffolk, which is a place that I love. I was also amongst people who had appreciated me for my endeavours on the football pitch and so there was always a good atmosphere about the place.

With a pub constantly full of Ipswich Town supporters, trade was always excellent and so I had plenty to keep me occupied, however everyone always wanted to buy me a drink. Where I had once drank to excess to escape the reality that my football career was over. I now drank to be sociable and to help keep the punters coming in. It could be argued that I might have displayed more will-power, however I won't be the first manager of a pub to fall into this trap and I'm sure I won't be the last.

You don't realise what is happening at first, however slowly but surely my consumption of alcohol was steadily increasing. From the minute we opened the doors in the morning, until we closed them on an evening, there was one customer after another and there was always someone who wanted a drink with me.

Someone would come in and he seems like a nice bloke and you are getting on well with him, you may well have made his day as he was a big fan of yours. You are enjoying each others company and he offers you a drink. It seems rude not to accept, besides what harm is a drink going to do? Before you know it, another customer joins you and then another. You are all having a good time and you know your income is dependent on keeping these people happy. One drink becomes two, which soon becomes three and so on. Before long you have been drinking all day and are out of your mind on the stuff.

Alternatively you may have had a bad day, one of those days when everything is going wrong. The delivery man is late, one of the beer pumps isn't working then the cleaner doesn't turn in for work. As the stress levels inside you build, a punter comes in and he approaches. You see a puzzled look on his face as he works out where he knows you from.

Suddenly it dawns on him: 'It's Kevin Beattie isn't it?' he asks. Before you have a chance to answer, he hits you with it: 'You were a great footballer, it was such a tragedy that you had to pack in so early.' You know he means well, but his innocent remark has sent you over the edge and by now your nerves are jangling.

The solution to take the edge of things is right before your eyes and again you hit the bottle.

Whilst I was in Norway, I was in a similar environment, however there were important differences. Firstly, I was largely prohibited from drinking due to the expensive nature of the prices, I couldn't afford to drink as much nor could people afford to buy me drinks. Secondly, whilst I also spent the working day talking with punters about football in Norway, it was about the game on a general level rather than about my own career.

In contrast, I now found that whenever the conversation turned to football, which it invariably did, it soon turned to my own career. 'You were a great player,' 'You should have won a hundred caps for England,' 'You were the best player I ever saw,' 'You should still be playing now,' and the worst one of all, 'Why aren't you playing now?' It was a question to which I still hadn't worked out the answer, although there was an easy escape route from facing up to answering it.

If I was feeling down and wanted to feel better or if I was feeling good and wanted to celebrate, I was surrounded by alcohol and had twenty-four hour, seven day a week access to it, three hundred and sixty five days a year. It seemed that every day I was drinking for one reason or another. At first I drank pints of lager, but after a while I found I couldn't keep downing them as they made me feel bloated. I soon started drinking hard liquor and vodka was my tipple, unfortunately after a time it became more than that, it also became my God.

When you are in a pub all day, you lose track of time and as the whole environment is about selling alcohol, you don't look out of place with a glass of the hard stuff in your hand. You also don't realise that you go from having a drink to escape from reality, to having a drink to actually help you get out of bed and function. I was soon drinking at least an entire bottle of vodka a day, although more often than not I was drinking far in excess of that. I was in the grip of an addiction and of course when that happens nothing else matters.

Things were complicated further when the owners of the pub said that the till was light and pointed the finger at me and Maggie. Some of the locals had warned us that it might happen as the two previous management couples had gone the same way. For a time I was suspended on full pay, which although meant I still had a wage coming in, didn't make me feel good, as I didn't like to be accused of doing something I hadn't done. However, it also meant that I was back to an empty day and the drinking escalated even further. I would estimate that at this point I was going through nearly two bottles of vodka a day.

Things soon got sorted out at the pub and my name was cleared, but mindful of the accusations I decided to move on and I took a similar management position at another pub in the town. Whilst it gave me a change of scenery it did not provide a change of routine. The same problems occurred and the drink was always there as an answer. Of course the very next day, you get out of bed and the same questions are asked of you again. You are on a slow steady treadmill to hell and you cannot get off.

I even lost interest in the game for a while. It had too many bad memories for me although of course it was impossible to fully get away from things. Not only was it the only thing that everyone wanted to talk to me about, the Portman Road stadium is based in the middle of the town and every day I had to go past it for some reason or another.

In the early days when he was the manager and most visitors

to the club would arrive by train, the 'Boss' was frequently asked for directions to the ground. His reply was always the same. 'Walk out of the station and open your eyes'. As anyone in the area will know, when you enter the town centre, the stadium is literally right before you. It stood as a constant reminder and for a time it hurt to see the place, as it made me realise how great my past had been and how bleak my future was.

As anyone who has worked in a pub will tell you, the job entails working long hours. So on top of drinking life-threatening amounts of alcohol, I never seemed to get a break, or find some quality time away from things. It was obvious that something had to give and only a matter of time before something serious happened to me. One evening after I had finished work, the inevitable occurred.

I was laid in bed half-asleep when I suddenly felt a terrible pain in my side, I had been drinking heavily and so was not at my best. When I tried to get up, I couldn't and I eventually collapsed in a heap on the floor. I had taken some painful knocks during my football career but I had never felt anything like this and I knew something serious was happening, Maggie picked up on this and was panicking and immediately called for an ambulance. I was by now in the most agonizing pain and I felt like somebody was stabbing me repeatedly in the side, I have never experienced pain like it before or since.

I was rushed to the hospital and in such pain that I was administered morphine and so don't remember too much about the next few days. I was placed into the intensive care unit and was apparently slipping in and out of consciousness. I was subjected to a series of tests and on first inspection, they thought that my appendix had burst, however further tests discovered that I had developed pancreatitis, which meant that my pancreas was basically giving up on me.

The pancreas is a vital organ which helps digest food and also produces insulin and mine had stopped working properly due to my excessive drinking. I was in a critical condition and literally fighting for my life. I was not responding to treatment and the medical team called in my family and told them to expect the worst. My parents couldn't even afford the train fare down from Carlisle so a terrible time was made even worse for them.

I obviously can't recall anything about it but one evening the family were told that I would not see out the night and I would be dead within twenty-four hours. The medical people don't give out a prognosis of that nature lightly and a local priest came to administer the last rites and everyone assumed that I was going to die. However I'm nothing if not a battler and I somehow made it through the night.

The medical people kept saying it was only a matter of time and that there was no hope for me but I kept surviving another day and then another and before long I had managed to last a few weeks. The hospital staff were amazed and said that they had no idea how I managed to pull through and that they had never seen anything like it before. In short, it was a minor miracle.

I remained in hospital and was still very ill, the medical staff knew that I was still very weak and still had the potential to relapse and ultimately die. However every day I lasted gave me a better chance of long-term survival and after sixteen weeks of hospital treatment, I was allowed to go home. I was still very poorly, I had entered the hospital weighing a burly sixteen stones and by the time I returned home I had lost seven stones in weight. I looked like someone who had been living in a concentration camp. Amazingly it was less than a decade since I had stopped playing football and I was still only thirty-seven years of age.

I was told that my next alcoholic drink could kill me. It was also said that I would be on medication for the rest of my life to help keep my pancreas in working order. For a long time, I wasn't able to do much except sit around the house and most of the time I was either in bed or on the sofa watching television. I really didn't have much interest in anything and I certainly had no interest in drinking, so a relapse back into my old ways was out of the question.

I didn't have any energy and it felt like an effort to even get out of bed in the morning, never mind leave the house and do something constructive with the day. Although I was determined to make a recovery as I knew that one or two vultures were circling and I was determined to prove them wrong.

I was fed up of reading bad things about myself in the press and I wanted to inspire some positive headlines for a change. I received a lot of letters of good-will which also helped and over the next year or so I built my strength up. I went for lots of walks and got plenty of fresh air and I forgot about the booze and physically and mentally got myself much better.

There was to be no lasting damage from the whole episode, apart from the fact that I have to take a couple of small white pills every day to ensure that my pancreas remains in working order. The medical staff were amazed that I hadn't become a diabetic, as a common side-effect of pancreatitis is that the patient is left with diabetes. However I didn't even contract that, although in the cruellest of ironies, with all the worry about my illness, my wife Maggie had herself become ill and was left with of all things diabetes – it is certainly a cruel and crazy world at times.

To help regain a bit of fitness, I began playing football for a team that represented a pub I had previously frequented. I was only in my late thirties and so was at an age when many players are still playing top-flight football. Indeed many players who I played with or against were still involved in the game. However at this stage of my life I was as far away from a professional career as is humanly possible.

I was amongst the piss-heads and wobbling beer-bellies unique to Sunday morning football, playing on bumpy pitches covered in pot-holes and dog shit. It was reminiscent of my early days back in Botcherby and my life in football had come full circle. Despite that, I quite enjoyed it and it was nice to help out the lads at the same time. Although after a few weeks of turning up and unbeknown to me, someone at the pub had invited an Anglia television crew down to film one of our games.

It coincided with me turning up not feeling my best, as with my pancreas ailment, it did not take much to get me feeling poorly. I wasn't going to play but I thought a run about might help sort me out. After ten minutes I was still feeling terrible, so much so that I was actually sick on the pitch. I felt humiliated as it was all captured on camera. I had once graced an FA Cup final and played for my country and I was now being sick on a scruffy park pitch whilst playing for some 'ragged arse rovers' style outfit.

I walked off the pitch and I was annoyed at myself for letting myself get into that position. I also felt that I had been set up and made to look stupid. I was obviously not at my best and I had no interest in capturing the lime-light, so I was angry that my below par performance had been turned into one for all and sundry to see.

I've got a pretty long fuse, but I let the manager know exactly what I thought about him. I had only been playing to help him out and regain a bit of fitness and I told him I wouldn't play for him again. In fact it was the last time I was to play in a competitive game of football anywhere. In many ways it was the least of my worries, the only things that I was qualified to do, was play football and work behind a bar. Now due to my various problems it seemed I could do neither.

Without work, times were very hard financially and as I obviously missed the big money that footballers get paid today, I had no alternative but to go and sign on the dole. It was very hard to do, but I'd paid my taxes and I couldn't see that I had any other option. It was still embarrassing though and it wasn't helped by the funny looks I received in the dole queue as people seemed to think I should be driving around in a big flash car and living in a mansion.

If I played today I no doubt would be, either way, it's no consolation when you haven't a penny to your name. Many of the people who worked in the dole office, or who were there claiming benefits were Ipswich Town fans and it wasn't unknown for me to be in the bizarre situation of turning up once a fortnight and being asked to sign autographs as well as sign for my giro cheque.

For a long time I used to sign on at an office close by to Portman Road, it was heart-breaking and certainly gave me plenty to think about. It was a stark reminder of how much my life had changed as I used to see former team-mates coming and going and their lives now seemed a million miles away from my own. I used to wonder how it had all ended up like this and whilst I accepted my own role in this downward spiral, it was still very hard to deal with.

My efforts to find other work weren't helped by my problems, as I suppose my issues with the drink were common knowledge and people think the worst and they don't want you around. Although I eventually got some bits and pieces of work, when I did some scouting at Norwich City, as well as finding similar work at Portsmouth where my good pal Alan Ball was the gaffer at the time.

The work was great but it was never enough to keep me going and as soon as a new manager arrives, the first thing he does is put his own men into a job so both positions never lasted too long. I also did some coaching work at non-league Clacton which was good fun, although in the end lack of finances at the club meant that I also had to leave that position.

I was soon offered work and a return to Portman Road, although it had nothing to do with the football club. Maggie and I had begun working as general help at a hotel based there. It was called a hotel but in reality it was more a bed and breakfast and it wasn't the most luxurious place by any means. Most of the guests were out of town building workers who stayed there during the week and then went home at the weekend. However things soon began to get busier and I noticed that a lot of single women were booking rooms for the weekend only.

The owners were pleased as they now had a full hotel seven days a week, although it didn't take long for me to work out what was going on. The girls were out of town prostitutes who were working the red light district based behind the football stadium. It has always been a seedy and unsavoury part of town and it made the headlines towards the end of 2006 when five women who worked the streets there were murdered.

Whilst I worked in the hotel, I turned a blind eye to things but when the girls started to bring back clients to the hotel it became another matter all together. When Maggie would go to the rooms the following morning and be presented with a floor full of used condoms that she was supposed to clean up, then that was the final straw. I wasn't prepared to have her work in an environment like that, so we handed in our notice and left.

You always assume that something will turn up, however nothing did and I had to go back on benefits. I was bringing up my family on about eighty pounds a week and it was an impossible task. My idea of a hot meal at this time was beans on toast. I had a television which needed a fifty pence piece placed inside it to make it work although I often couldn't find a coin to make it go. It also used to upset me that I couldn't give my kids the same little treats that other Dad's could.

It got so bad that I was even reduced to walking the streets and picking up cigarette butts that other people had thrown on the floor so that I could have a smoke. I felt that I had hit rock-bottom and I couldn't take anymore. I had started drinking again and found it hard to sort myself out. I couldn't see a way out of the mess that I was in and I could see no hope of things getting any better.

It seemed like everything was out of control and I had honestly had enough. I thought that my wife and kids would be better of without me and that if I was gone then they could have a better way of life. I was sat at home one afternoon and had a bottle of vodka and a bottle of sleeping pills beside me. For a while I'd often gone to bed and prayed that I wouldn't wake up, however I always did. I now wanted an end to it all and I thought that the only way I would get it was to give nature a helping hand. I was going to commit suicide.

I had worked my way through the booze and had popped some of the pills when there was a knock on the door – it was my old friend Bob Shelley. I hadn't seen Bob for some time as we had drifted apart. He told me later that he had got a sixth-sense that something was wrong and that he should come and visit me. I probably wasn't making much sense but I spoke with Bob at length and as a friend I told him what I was in the process of doing. I had already taken enough booze and pills to kill most people, but over the years I suppose my tolerance level for it all was more than that of most normal people. Bob stayed with me and he obviously talked me out of it. If he hadn't arrived, I am positive I would have seen it through, so in many ways he saved my life.

I had actually been thinking of attaching a hose pipe to the car but my car had been repossessed. I suppose all I could do was laugh and try and pull through it all. Often all you're left with is a bit of dignity and it seemed I wasn't even afforded that, as it was common knowledge that I was down and practically out. I subsequently did a piece with a national newspaper saying as much, which wasn't great having my dirty laundry aired in public, but as anyone who knew me was familiar with my situation, it hardly seemed to matter. It brought a few quid through the door and helped keep things going for a while and I suppose that's all that mattered.

It proved to be something of a turning point however I can't say that it has been a magic carpet ride since. Some days are better than others and I suppose that my life is the same as that of most other people, in that it has its good and bad moments. I have done what I could to scratch a living, I have had little odds and sods of work but mostly I have survived on disability benefits.

My knees are shot to pieces and I need joint replacements for them both. Where I was once one of the quickest professional footballers in the game, I now struggle to walk a few hundred yards. It has made it difficult to find work although I also admit that the drinking hasn't helped and it is something that has made me unreliable and also made me do things that I have regretted. However I'd like to think that I am a decent bloke at heart and that most people would say the same about me if asked.

A few years ago my own problems were made to look insignificant when Maggie was diagnosed with multiple sclerosis. She is a lovely person and it makes me wonder what she has done to deserve such a fate. However, we have been through so much and we shall get through this as well. It certainly helped me get my own act together as I need to be around to help her and I am essentially her full-time carer although Maggie's Sister Judith, her Mum Winnie and our three lovely girls: Emma, Sarah and Louise also do a great job in helping out.

It is often a mundane existence that I lead, so it was a lovely surprise when one day a few years ago I received a call from Roddy Collins who was the manager of Carlisle United at the time. He asked me if I would be interested in helping him a couple of days a week doing some coaching for him. Would I be interested? I would have walked there for the chance.

It was great to be involved again – especially with my home town club and although I never fulfilled my ambition of playing for them, this was the next best thing. Roddy was a terrific guy to work with and it was also a great thrill to meet his brother Steve, who popped by a couple of times. I have always loved boxing and still have great memories of watching him beat both Chris Eubank and Nigel Benn.

The club had been struggling for a few years and like most managers, Roddy was working on a tight budget and so always faced something of an uphill task. However there was a lovely atmosphere at the club, with some great people there and I personally enjoyed every minute of it all. The results on the park were mixed, although whilst I was there we reached the 2002/3 LDV vans trophy final at the Millennium Stadium, although unfortunately we lost the game 2-0 against Bristol City.

Although we were beaten, after the game the booze was flowing and caught in good company, I started to sink a few. I was enjoying myself, causing no one else any harm and letting off steam, as most people up and down the country do every evening of the week. As long as I stick to a few beers I am ok, but on this occasion I was getting stuck into the hard stuff and the next morning, I woke up with not only a banging headache but a terrible pain in my side. I knew immediately what the problem was and I got myself over to the hospital.

I was released the next day and I resolved to be careful in the future. I was sorry for putting the hospital staff to any trouble and there was no real harm done. I was just upset that it had occurred whilst part of a club fixture. Although I have to say that most of the people there had enjoyed a good evening out and had sunk more than their fair share of booze, so it wasn't just me who had gone over the top.

I felt that given time we could have turned the club around although the results went against us and Roddy eventually lost his job, which also signalled the end of the road for me as well. Fortunately not long afterwards, I was given the opportunity to go to the USA helping a friend who coached school children. I thoroughly enjoyed it and I really got my head down, I stayed off the booze, got myself fit and felt really good about things. It was lovely to see the youngsters improve their game and the group I was responsible for ended up winning their league.

I would have loved to have stayed on, but unfortunately it was only ever going to be a temporary situation. It made me wish that I had taken all the necessary coaching badges, as it seems that without those obtaining any coaching work is difficult. Especially when you combine that with the Chinese whispers regarding my drinking that often precede me when ever I apply for any type of work.

I haven't done much coaching work since, although I did do a short spell for Barry Fry at Peterborough. I would love to have another crack at things somewhere and would especially like to work with a junior side, as when they are that age, you can make a really positive difference and help get them into good habits. I feel that I can help not only with my experience obtained as a player, but also keep people away from a few of the pitfalls that I eventually fell into myself.

It was around this time that I suffered another health scare, when one evening after watching a game at Portman Road, I went home feeling a bit light headed. I also had pins and needles down one side of my body and as soon as I got home I went to bed. I woke up in the middle of the night and I felt terrible, I was covered in red blotches and found it difficult to move. Maggie rang for an ambulance, although when I arrived in hospital, no one was sure what the problem was, so I was kept there for a couple of days as a precautionary measure.

It was later diagnosed that I had suffered a minor stroke. Fortunately I had suffered no side-effects and no lasting damage, so I guess I was very lucky. It sounds like a frightening prognosis, but compared to the pancreas situation, it was nothing and within a day or two of arriving home I felt fine and have never suffered since. As with the pancreas, I amazed the medical staff who couldn't believe that I had no lasting damage. I can only assume that it is to do with the fact that when I was playing football I was an extremely fit person.

It is in many ways ironic, as apart from my Mum who passed away when at a good age my family has a habit of dying young and before their time. The sense of irony was added to by the fact that I was able to overcome an illness that would have killed most people, yet I was unable to overcome the problems with my knees, that ended my career all those years ago.

The only other scare I have suffered since, occurred when a good friend of mine – journalist Dave Allard wrote to the FA on my behalf and subsequently managed to get a few of the caps replaced that I had lost in the fire in Norway. He also contacted the PFA, who organised a presentation on the pitch at Portman Road for me during the 2005/6 season where I was due to receive a replica trophy of my PFA Young Player of the year award that had also been destroyed.

On the day of the ceremony I was picked up by Dave and another journalist Mel Henderson and I was looking forward to things. As is normal I had to take a couple of tablets for my pancreas, which I need to take every day to make sure that the pancreas functions properly. It was set to be a proud day, although from the moment I arrived with Mel and Dave at Portman Road, I honestly don't remember a thing.

Apparently I collapsed in the VIP area and was checked out by the club doctor and they couldn't work out what was wrong with me. I wasn't feeling very well although I wasn't bad enough to require hospital treatment so I was put in a taxi and sent home. What was most embarrassing was the fact that whilst all this was occurring, a presentation party from the PFA were waiting to give me my award in front of 25,000 plus Ipswich Town supporters.

The presentation had been well advertised, so I suppose people wondered what had happened and obviously the rumour mill was soon in full effect. I was pissed, I never turned up, by the end of the following week, I had heard them all. Although I honestly don't know what occurred, maybe a combination of the tablets and the adrenaline inspired by the occasion got the better of me.

I also suppose that as I have damaged my body over the years, every now and then it may temporarily give up on me. I was told I wouldn't see out the night nearly twenty years ago, so whilst it's not something I would wish for, I guess I can't complain too much if it happens. Both Mel and Dave will confirm that when I met them I was sober and I had no chance to get into the state I was in through drink. I was upset that one or two people were thinking the worst about me again, but I guess in the past I have let people down through drink, so I can't complain if people assume I had done it again. A couple of days later I apologised to Mick McGuire at the PFA and he was fine about things and I eventually got my trophy from Ipswich Town chairman David Sheepshanks, in a private ceremony in front of friends and family.

It is in many ways a strange life that I lead, as at one level I am an average person who lives in Ipswich and does his best to make ends meet. Yet to other people, I am a football idol and so still get asked for my autograph. It is a life of highs and lows that's for sure which are often encapsulated in a single day. For example I remember once having to sign on for my disability money and then heading to the PFA awards in London.

It was the 25th anniversary since I became the first man to win the young player of the year award and there I was seated at the top table, suited and booted, meeting people like Dennis Bergkamp and Michael Owen. I haven't always enjoyed talking about my football career, as it often brought back bad memories regarding the way it all ended, but over the years I have gradually come to terms with things.

On this occasion it was a privilege to be invited to such a prestigious event and many people were saying very complimentary things about me. It was lovely to hear this, as it was all coming from fellow players and people who I admired myself. It was a terrific evening and a reminder that as well as some difficult times, my life has had some wonderful moments.

On another occasion, I woke up to find a pile of letters on the doormat and there amongst the usual junk mail and bills, was an envelope with a House of Lords seal on the front. I opened it up and found it was from Lord Richard Ryder who it turned out was a government chief whip. He went on to say that he was a great Ipswich Town fan and asked if there was any chance of meeting me. We eventually met and whilst I didn't think that we would have too much in common, I found him to be a really down to earth guy. We have since become good friends and I still meet up with him occasionally, which is something that I enjoy doing.

Perhaps the most bizarre call I received, came a couple of years ago when I was contacted by a journalist from Manchester who said he believed that he had something that belonged to me. I hadn't a clue what he was talking about, but it turned out that he had a ring that Maggie had once given to me, which had been stolen thirty years previously.

We had been playing at Manchester United and whilst the game was in progress, the dressing rooms had been broken into.

A few of the players had some money stolen and personal possessions taken. Somewhat bizarrely they had also helped themselves to a set of false teeth that belonged to Roger Osborne.

Dave Sexton, who was the manager of Manchester United at the time, was really upset about it all. He vowed to do all he could, but in the end we never got our belongings back. I had a lovely gold ring which had a ruby stone in the middle stolen. It was made worse by the fact that it had great personal value to me as it was given to me by Maggie. With so many years having passed, I had obviously given up hope on ever getting it back.

It turned out that the journalist had been having a weekend away in Spain, when he had become involved in a conversation with another holiday-maker. They were both football fans and so soon struck up a bit of rapport over a few beers. As the drinking escalated, the other guy began to get a little downcast and declared that he didn't want to talk about football anymore as his only regret in life was a football related incident. The journalist was confused, but as his profession would suggest, he was a naturally curious person and he eventually got the other guy to confess all.

He admitted that as a young boy he had managed to get into the dressing rooms at Old Trafford and had stolen personal items from the players. It had played on his conscience and with each passing year, he felt worse about it. The guy could even remember that on the day in question that it was a Manchester United v Ipswich Town fixture. He had even kept the gold ring and eventually agreed to hand it over to the journalist.

The journalist set to work and began unearthing a few old photographs and eventually he found one where I was wearing the ring. When he got in touch with me, I thought he was joking, but it was a lovely surprise to get the ring back and I wear it proudly to this day. Unfortunately for Roger he wasn't quite so lucky and he never did get his false teeth back.

Another immensely pleasing moment came when I won a poll amongst the fans, as to who was the greatest ever Ipswich Town player. I did so by obtaining twice as many votes as anyone else. When I think of some of the great players who have played for the club, then it is a wonderful honour to have received and I really appreciate that my efforts are valued by the supporters. As far as I am concerned, they are the most important people at any club and if I am appreciated and valued by them, then that will do for me.

It was especially gratifying as there is no bigger fan of the club than I am and I will always be blue and white at heart. I never actually wanted to play my club football anywhere else although there were many off the record offers to do so from clubs both at home and abroad. However the 'Boss' always rejected them all out of hand and in the end clubs knew that they were wasting their time even asking.

The only formal offer the club received was when Gordon Milne, who was at the time the manager of Coventry City, put in an offer of £450,000 for me. I knew Gordon as he had been the team manager when I had represented England as part of the 'Little World Cup' and whilst I thought he was a decent guy, I was never tempted to leave Portman Road. At the time the record British transfer fee stood at the £500,000 that West Bromwich Albion had paid Middlesbrough for David Mills. The 'Boss' told Gordon that his offer would buy my right leg, which was something of a gentle dig at him, as everyone knew I was a predominantly left-footed player.

I still go to Portman Road and love to be around the place, I kick every ball, my legs are twitching, my arms are shaking and I still want to get out there. I am always envious of whoever is wearing the number six shirt and I still wish that it was me who was playing. It is a unique atmosphere there and it is a really homely place, which still retains that touch of class which was instilled into the club through the Cobbold family.

I have helped out on the corporate side of things on behalf of the club and a couple of years ago was also pleased to get the chance to offer my assistance as a co-commentator to Terry Baxter at BBC Radio Suffolk. Dubbed 'The Beat and The Bax', it was lovely to get to travel about and see plenty of games and visit different stadiums, where I would often bump into old pals from my playing days.

I got to meet the 'Boss' when he was at Newcastle and ex-England colleagues like Peter Taylor when he was at Leicester City. I also spent plenty of time in the company of big Joe Royle when he was the manger at the club. I knew him through the England set up and he remains a terrific guy. Joe had been left with mobility problems as like me had suffered with knee problems. He eventually had a knee replacement operation and said he felt like a different man. I have been in touch with the PFA and hope to finally get my own knees sorted out.

I didn't actually earn anything for doing the radio work, but it wasn't about money, I really enjoyed being involved. I have never enjoyed pundits who sit on the proverbial fence and it was great to be asked to give my opinion. I tried to give an honest viewpoint and it seemed to go down well, although it occasionally got me into trouble. For example, I remember making a few comments that didn't go down well with my old team-mate George Burley when he was the manager at the club.

It was innocuous enough stuff in my opinion, as I merely passed comment on both team and tactical selection, which as I saw it was what I was there to do. I'm not sure whether George felt that as an old team-mate I shouldn't be critical in public of him, but there was no malice on my part and I was merely speaking as someone who played the game and wanted to see Ipswich Town doing well. Fortunately we soon resolved our differences and our little disagreement got smoothed over.

When Ipswich played against Inter Milan during a UEFA Cup tie, I got into trouble when Terry asked me for my opinion about some of the gamesmanship that was going on. I was getting a bit annoyed and so reacted by saying that I was sick of the 'Eye-ties' and also commentated on the fact that they always seemed to be diving about all the time. There were a number of complaints and a few people were upset, apparently it was the use of the phrase 'Eye-ties' which had got up some people's noses. There was no malice on my part, as far as I can tell it's just a shortened version of the word Italian in the same way that the word 'Brit' is short for British. If I'd said 'Brit' then I'm sure that no one would have batted an eyelid.

One good thing that came of the Inter Milan incident was that the amount of listeners went up. I'm sure that half of them were listening to see what I might say next but that was fine by me and for a time the station bosses were really happy. Just as I thought that things were going well, there was a change of management at the station and the first thing that they did was get some new people involved and this signalled the end of 'The Beat and the Bax' partnership.

As an experienced media man, Terry was able to get a job as the director of media and communication at Ipswich Town, unfortunately for me, it's a bit harder to find something when you're an ex-footballer with bad knees. It was a shame as it was a job of work which I really enjoyed. Since then I'm always getting stopped by people who ask when I'm going back on the radio and the simple answer to that is whenever I'm asked to.

I was particularly incensed about what went on during the Inter Milan game, as diving is a particular part of the game that I hate. Anyone who deliberately tries to get a fellow professional dismissed has no place in football. I personally went to the FA headquarters to appeal against a booking given against Ron Futcher who was then a Luton Town striker as he faced a suspension, for a tackle that he had put in on me. I felt that Ron was unlucky to get his yellow-card and so I went to the hearing to speak on his behalf. This was despite the fact that it was on a bank holiday weekend and at the time of a rail strike, so the traffic into London was horrendous.

However it was something I felt strongly about and I wanted to see something done about that aspect of the game, as I still do now. Like most people I enjoy seeing two teams going at it and whilst I also like to see skill and guile displayed, I especially enjoy the physical confrontation between a striker and a central defender. I am not talking about crude or dirty challenges here, just hard but fair physical play.

I obviously played in an era when some of the toughest players in the game were plying their trade and every time that I pulled on my boots, I expected a hard physical contest and that I would have a battle on my hands for the full ninety minutes. I expected my opponent to do whatever he could to unsettle me and within the rules of the game I would return him the same compliment. After the game, I would happily shake his hand and buy him a beer and there were no grudges whatsoever.

I remember that during one game Joe Jordan, who was a fearsome competitor, knocked out four of my teeth following an aerial challenge when he elbowed me in the mouth. Joe later apologised and said it was an accident and I took him at his word and there were no hard feelings. However, it was important that I put out the message to him and anyone else, that I was no soft touch and when we next played I made sure that I hit Joe with a peach of a tackle.

It was very hard but fair and rocked every bone in Joe's body and he did not finish the game. I had not fouled him or deliberately set out to hurt him, merely show him that I was a competitor and that I was every bit as hard as he was. After the game I saw Joe and we had a beer and looked forward to our next confrontation. It wasn't always as extreme as that, however football should always have an element to it, which involves strong physical play, by guys who get stuck in and give their all.

With regard to my own career, I am often asked if mine is a hard-luck story one of unfulfilled potential and self-inflicted difficulty which should have seen me take a different path. I have to admit that in some ways it is although I try not to look at it that way and take some positives from it all. I would certainly have loved to have been able to have played football for a few years longer and to have seen how far I could have gone. To have extended my career at Ipswich and won a few more trophies and to have played more for my country would have been lovely, although sadly it was not meant to be.

Whenever that letter from the FA asking me to play for England arrived at the club, I used to tingle with excitement at the prospect of pulling on that famous white jersey. The lads would often hide the letters and kid me that I hadn't been picked, although eventually they didn't need to hide anything, as the letters would arrive and I would have to turn the opportunity down due to injury. I lost count of how many times this happened and I would subsequently watch the game on television and think that I should be there.

During my first three seasons in football, I felt indestructible as I played every week and had soon racked up over one hundred and fifty appearances for the club. The awards and plaudits flooded in and it all seemed very easy. I then started to encounter misfortune and I suppose if there was any bad luck about it did come way. It wasn't always the serious stuff such as the burns or the knee injuries. I can remember feeling fine all week and then on the eve of an England game coming down with a throat virus that had me laid up in bed and forced me to miss the game.

If I did play, I often carried a knock or had something that prevented me from feeling 100%. I can remember during another England game, playing with a huge cyst on the inside of my face which was so big that it left me unable to close my mouth. I got fed up with it and remember that I had it lanced at half-time. The pain was incredible and wasn't helped when in the second half someone elbowed me in the exact area where the cyst had been.

It seemed that if anyone was to twist an ankle or come down with the flu it always seemed to be me, although of course the more serious injuries and accidents came later, the burns, the car crashes, there wasn't much that didn't come my way. How much of it was bad luck and how much was inspired by my own behaviour, I'll leave for others to decide, maybe I was blessed and cursed as some people have suggested.

I think that with the advances in medical technology and with football now being such big business, I may well have had my career saved. It is something I have thought about many times and it has caused me great anguish over the years. I know that a number of modern-day players have had serious knee injuries and managed to recover.

I understand that key-hole surgery is something that helps, it is not so invasive and so the operation is much less traumatic. Ironically the pioneer of this style of surgery was Dr David Dandy, the man who gave me the verdict that it was all over. My own operations were very different, as I had the traditional surgery, where the skin on the knee joint was cut open and as a result, I have huge scars down the side of each knee which are several inches long. My right knee in particular resembles a snakes and ladders board. Obviously repeatedly cutting open the flesh on a knee joint isn't going to do it any good and I think that this definitely contributed to my own demise, however in those days the technology was not there to do it any other way.

Whether coming back so soon after my first operation had a bearing on subsequent events, is something I really don't know about. On the face of it, to be playing only three weeks after an operation seems bizarre. However I wanted to play, the club wanted me to play and the fans wanted me to play, so it seemed to be the best decision all around.

In the end, for whatever reason, it wasn't to be and I couldn't ever recapture the sharpness which I enjoyed in my early career. I don't why, or how this should be, all I know is that after a great deal of soul-searching, I have eventually come to accept that it is a hypothetical situation and a waste of time worrying about it.

On the issue of cortisone, if I had my time again, I would not have had the injections. I think that it is like asbestos and thalidomide, in that they are products that have been shown to have serious side effects and the passage of time has shown that they should not be used in the way that they were. A number of players have considered taking legal action regarding cortisone but in reality there is no one to sue. It all boils down to the issue of negligence and nobody who authorised or administered giving us cortisone was negligent. It was given and accepted in good faith and it was only many years later that there was found to be any kind of problem.

I don't believe that it is so much the use of cortisone, as much as the repeated use of it, as well as someone injecting directly into your joint which causes the problems. I did have someone tell me that two or three cortisone injections in a lifetime are sufficient for anyone. I had that many to get me through the FA Cup final alone. There were of course many more besides that and I honestly can't remember how many times I had an injection to help get me through a game. I attach no blame to anyone though and feel that they were given to players without anyone knowing what the consequences would eventually be.

I did appear on a television show for the 'Trevor Macdonald Tonight' series entitled 'Cortisone Eleven'. It investigated the cases of several players from my era and how we all suffered mobility problems from having received the injections. In many ways it was also an insight into how difficult many players found it adapting to life after football.

I remember after filming that we were taken to a room to relax and unwind and on a large table there was a buffet and bottles of wine laid on for us. I wasn't interested in the food but as I was in the midst of my own drinking problems the wine certainly looked very appealing. Stood beside me, was the former

Chelsea striker Ian Hutchinson who had also appeared on the programme.

Ian's career had in many ways mirrored my own, as he had to finish early due to injury. He had also won a FA Cup winners medal and he now also seemed to be struggling to adapt to life without football. As we both waited for someone to arrive with a bottle opener, Ian grabbed a spoon and proceeded to open the wine bottle with it. I looked at him in amazement, he just looked back at me and shrugged his shoulders, 'Practice' he said blankly. He offered no explanation but did not need to either as we both understood what it meant.

We had a drink together and I wished Ian well. I knew exactly what he was going through, as I also lived through it every day. I was extremely sorry to hear that not too long afterwards Ian passed away, he was a good man and deserved better. I suppose you can get wrapped up in your own problems and not realise that other people are experiencing similar difficulties as well.

I remember some years previously being on an overseas tour to Canada and the USA and I met up with an old pal from the England set-up Dave Clement. Dave was a smashing footballer and a lovely guy and on the surface seemed to have a great life so it was one hell of a shock when I heard a few years later that he had committed suicide.

Looking back, I wish that I had the sort of advice available that players get today. I am not a particularly well organised person and have never being good at handling money and it may have meant that I had more to show for my career. A good example of this is illustrated when I was offered the chance to buy the club house that I was living in at a discount rate. Instead I bought my next-door neighbours house in a private sale for a much higher price. Don't ask me why, I suppose I have a habit of doing things that I shouldn't always do.

I did actually have an agent for a short time whilst I was playing. It was a rarity in those days as players tended to get what they were offered and any commercial activities extended to things like a free car, or possibly opening a supermarket for a few extra quid. I was approached by this guy who told me he was starting a new agency and asked me if I would be interested in signing up with him. He looked the part and said the right things so I gave him a go.

A few weeks later I got a knock on the door from the police. They showed me a photograph and asked me if I recognised the man in the picture. He didn't instantly look like a man at all, as he was wearing a woman's wig and a dress. However underneath all the get up with a big smile on his face was my new agent. It turned out that not only was he a secret transvestite but he was also a con artist, as he had been ripping people off and that's why the police were chasing him.

I had to laugh, as added to the sponsored car fiasco, it seemed like I was cursed when it came to any extra-curricular activity. So after that, when anybody asked me about getting involved in anything I said no. It was another scenario in a long line of things that I regret and wished had worked out differently, although I try to be positive about my career and focus on the fact that people obviously rated me as a football player.

I am sure that I have provided people with immense enjoyment and possibly an escape from their own troubles for ninety minutes on a Saturday afternoon which is something that I am proud of. I always found things very easy on a football pitch and I think that is what most impressed other people. I would like to think that I was also an honest player, whose playing career was based on upon a bed-rock of commitment and hard-work and that what skill and ability I had, I used to its full potential.

In saying that the years have rolled by and it is amazing how quickly time has passed and it is now over twenty years since my career finished. I still have the memories and I occasionally see people from the good old days. It is good to catch up and I always enjoy meeting them. I always enjoy seeing the 'Boss,' who remains as ever, a great character. One of the last times I saw him, was when he was promoting his own book over in Great Yarmouth, where he was signing some copies as part of an appearance at a question and answer session in the town.

I went to see him with my good pal Dave Allard and before he was due to appear on stage we checked into the hotel he was booked into. It was lovely to see him, but before we left for the evening out, we were asked whether we required a breakfast for the following morning. I ordered a full English, Dave ordered kippers, whilst the 'Boss' said he would leave it and wait until the next day.

The next morning, the 'Boss' had another function to attend and so was up and away before us, leaving Dave and I to have breakfast together. We told the waiter that we had ordered our food the night before and my full English duly arrived. A few minutes later, the waiter again arrived, however instead of Dave's breakfast he arrived with a sheepish look on his face. It turned out that the reason for his look was that when he arrived for his breakfast earlier the 'Boss' had said he fancied some kippers. However the only kippers in the place were the ones that Dave had pre-ordered.

It's not every day that someone who is both a knight of the

realm and a former England football team manager arrives in town and if he wants kippers for breakfast, then that is what he will surely get, come what may. To be fair to the waiter, he could have given Dave a lame excuse about the lack of kippers, instead he gave it to him straight, 'Sir Bobby wanted kippers and there were only two left,' he said with a shrug of his shoulders, which left Dave in no uncertain terms as to where he stands in the pecking order.

Like a lot of former players, I am often asked about the wages that the stars of today earn. It would be very nice to have a salary of £100,000 per year, never mind earn that a week and it is a mind-blowing amount of money to be on. I suppose that football players have always earned decent money but people doing a job such as a doctor earned more than I did when I played. Some would say rightly so and would also add that a situation where a footballer earns more in a week, than a doctor earns in a year is unjust and it would be very hard to argue against that.

However I do think that anyone who was offered the money would take it and anyone who said any different would be lying. The only thing that I object to is that a very ordinary player can now be earning a fortune and will probably walk away with more money in a week, than I did in a decade. I can't see how anyone can justify that.

The best money I earned from football actually came during the brief spell I played at Barnet, which is a bizarre thought, as at the time they were a non-league side. When I was at Middlesbrough they also seemed to be throwing the money around, which was somewhat ironic as not long afterwards they went bust. I suppose it is pointless wondering about what might have been although it is fair to say that a couple of seasons at the top and the lads of today are set for life and even the most reckless of players would find it hard to end up penniless and in the state that I have found myself in as they simply earn so much money now.

They also receive the best advice, have the best management companies working on their behalf and are in many ways mini-industries that provide a living for a lot of other people. Whether I would have adapted to this I am not too sure as I liked to keep things nice and simple. All I liked to do was turn-up, pull on my boots and then after the game, head off and have a few beers.

Whilst the money would have been nice, I still had a wonderful time and got to travel and to see places I can only have imagined of. The best thing of all was being paid to do something I genuinely loved doing. The only regret I have is that I wished it could have lasted longer and that my career hadn't ended so prematurely.

I see the facilities at Ipswich now and they are fantastic, even the young lads there have a lot to be thankful for. They are called academy scholars – not apprentices now and they are treated better than many professional players were in my day. They don't see a dust pan and brush and if a coach or manager gave them the kind of bollocking that I was witness to, then they'd probably end up in court.

I can remember the likes of Cyril Lea and later Bobby Ferguson having to shout and bawl at people, but nobody thought any less of them – quite the opposite. Whilst they had to play the sergeant-major role, they were also often something of a surrogate Dad to the younger lads and were always there if you needed them. Although they had to let you know in no uncertain terms if you had stepped out of line, they were also great blokes, fantastic coaches and had the respect of everyone at the club. It does disappoint me when I meet young lads and even worse their parents and all they seem to be obsessed about is the amount of money that they could be making. I might be old-fashioned but to me your only motivation should be about playing football. If you get that right, everything else will follow naturally.

Some people even complain about the amount of games that are played now, but such was my love for the game, that in my early days at Ipswich Town, I sometimes played for the youth team on a Saturday morning and the reserve team on a Saturday afternoon. I wanted to play every day of the week and become the best football player I possibly could.

I must have done something right as upon my arrival at Ipswich I was referred to in the press as a 'gangly rough-hewn youngster' and they were probably right. Yet within a year the same people were describing me as the new Bobby Moore. I would have loved to have achieved what Bobby did and won over 100 caps for my country and lifted the World Cup but my injuries made that particular quest impossible.

I would also loved to have been known as the best player England ever had however if I am to be called the best player England never had, then I will take that as a compliment. More importantly, I'd like to think that when all is said and done, when people talk about me, they won't remember the bad luck and the injuries. I also hope that they will forgive me my errors of judgement and my problems and difficulties and they will think about me in one way. All I ask is that I am remembered as someone who loved to play football and was the best player that he could possibly be.

AND FINALLY

I am often asked about who my favourite players were and to pick a team from the players that I both played with and against. I was fortunate to come into contact with some great players and if you count my 'Escape to Victory' performance, I could even lay claim to having played alongside the great Pele. I did play against players of the calibre of Johan Cruyff and Michel Platini, although I have limited my selections to players that I came into contact with on a regular basis.

I have picked two teams, one featuring players who at one time or another I played with, the other team is picked from players that I only ever played against. It was a tough task and there were many excellent players who didn't make the list, however I think that they make for two superb teams and I hope that you enjoy reading the reasons for my selections.

TEAM-MATES

The following is a team picked from players that I was fortunate to have lined up alongside either on international duty for England, or on club duty at Ipswich Town. Some I only had the pleasure of playing with a few times, whilst others I lined up with hundreds of times. Either way it was a pleasure to have been in the same side as them all.

(Goal-keeper) Peter Shilton
I only played briefly with Peter for England, when both he and Ray Clemence were being rotated for the number one spot, which

I always found to be a strange situation. Ray was an excellent player too, but I think that Peter just had the edge on him. He wasn't the tallest 'keeper but still had a presence about him which is always reassuring to defenders. He was a very vocal player and always seemed to be shouting out instructions and organising his players which was something I liked, as you knew where you stood with a player like that. Peter's forte was that he was an outstanding shot-stopper and he was also an incredibly fit and agile player. That he played into his forties and made over 1000 appearances, tells you all you need to know about how great a player Peter was.

(Right-back) George Burley

I played alongside George on many occasions for Ipswich Town and he was a very neat and tidy player who did the simple things well. I think that players like George, who keep things nice and easy are sometimes taken for granted, as they often don't catch the eye as much as the flamboyant players who grab the headlines. However I always appreciated George for being a solid hard-working player, who turned in consistent performances. George made 500 appearances for Ipswich Town and I wouldn't imagine that too many of those were games where he didn't turn in a solid performance that let nobody down. For me there are not too many players that can say that they managed that.

(Left-back) Mick Mills

Mick was a brilliant captain for both Ipswich Town and England, who led by example and didn't ask anyone to do something he wasn't willing to do himself. Mick was comfortable on either flank and was a very solid and dependable player who made very few mistakes. Like George Burley, he was a player who did the simple things well and didn't try and complicate it by trying to do anything that didn't need doing. Mick was happy to get involved when the muck and bullets were flying and was the kind of guy that you wanted alongside you in the trenches. Mick made 734 appearances for Ipswich Town, which is an amazing record and testimony to not only his great fitness but also his consistency of performance.

(Centre-back) Allan Hunter

I played alongside Allan for most of my career at Ipswich Town and such was our understanding that the 'Boss' labelled us 'Bacon and Eggs'. Allan was already an established and experienced player when I arrived on the scene and it was brilliant to have him alongside me as I made my way in the game. He taught me a lot about football and I will always be grateful to him for that. People often talk about the hard-men of the game and there were few harder than Allan. Nobody took any liberties with him and he was just the type of guy you wanted with you on a freezing cold afternoon when the challenges were flying in and it was time to stand up and be counted. Allan never let anyone down and for me he is an absolute legend.

(Centre-back) Colin Todd

Colin was a classy performer who could play football and also stop others from doing the same, which is a perfect combination for a central defender. There wasn't too much that seemed to faze Colin and whether you wanted to play football or have a battle, he was happy to oblige either way. A lot of defenders aren't very comfortable on the ball and are only really 'destroyers' who can stop the opposition. Colin was more than that and the type of player who when he stopped an opposition attack, immediately looked to start something creative for his own team, which is they way it should be as far as I am concerned. Colin's gift was making that aspect of the game look easy, which of course it isn't.

(Right-midfield) Alan Ball

I played alongside Alan for England, which was a great privilege as he was a bit of a hero to me, as I had seen him winning the World Cup final when I was a boy. Alan was a bundle of energy and a very dynamic player who worked tirelessly for the team. It's now very normal to have a midfield player who is able to get up and down the pitch from box to box for ninety minutes. However Alan was doing this a long time before most players and in many ways he was ahead of his time. He was a great player, who was able to create things and make things happen, but also get his foot in and win a tackle and stop the other team playing. Alan is also a very bubbly personality and his enthusiasm rubbed off on everyone and he was a tremendous person to be around both on and off the pitch.

(Centre-midfield) Colin Bell

Colin wasn't nicknamed 'Nijinsky' for nothing and he was a thoroughbred performer and a tremendous athlete, who seemed to get around the pitch with the greatest of ease. Colin was totally comfortable on the ball and had lovely balance and movement and was a natural player who made it all look very easy – which of course it isn't. It was a tragedy that like me, Colin had to retire prematurely through injury. He was a wonderful player and when I made the step-up into the international scene it was by watching players like Colin that made me realise that I was now operating at another level.

(Centre-midfield) John Wark

It is a credit to how good a player John was, by the fact that I could have picked him in any number of positions. He was an extremely versatile player and was highly effective as a sweeper, midfielder and also as a striker. He was a very composed player who was comfortable on the ball and he could read the game as well as anyone that I played with or against. John was a superb defender who was able to play until he was nearly forty years of age, but was also brilliant at getting forward and had an uncanny knack of scoring goals. He scored nearly 200 during his career and often played in the back four, which tells you all that you need to know about what a superb player he was.

(Left-midfield) Arnold Muhren

Arnold was a class act who once prompted BBC commentator John Motson to name him 'The man with velvet feet' and he had an especially cultured left-foot that could ping inch-perfect passes all over the park. He was brought up in the traditions of the great Ajax football club and so from an early age, he was taught to play football in what I would describe as the right way. Arnold was a very intelligent footballer and he wasn't one to be lumping aimless passes all over the place. He was a very graceful performer and I think it is people such as Arnold who have helped make football known as the beautiful game.

(Centre-forward) Paul Mariner

I would rate Paul as one of the best pieces of business that Ipswich Town have ever done and he was an absolute bargain at the £220,000 fee it cost to sign him from Plymouth Argyle. 'PM' was equally comfortable with the ball in the air and at his feet and he was a very solid and dependable player who could take the stick that was dished out by tough-nut defenders, of whom there were many. He always chipped in with his fair share of goals although he was also an unselfish player, who was a great foil for other strikers such as Eric Gates and Alan Brazil. 'PM' was also capped by England 35 times scoring 14 goals, which tells you that he could not only do the business at club level but at international level too.

(Centre-forward) Kevin Keegan

Kevin was a bundle of energy and was a very hard-working player who turned himself into one of the best players in the game. Kevin was a bit like one of those annoying little Yorkshire terriers and I mean that as a compliment, in that he was always snapping away and whatever you did to him, he wouldn't go away. He would be running and chasing and harrying for the full ninety minutes and he never gave you a minute of peace. I played against Kevin many times during my career and he always made it difficult for me. It was therefore a nice change to line up alongside him for the England team. Getting to train and play alongside Kevin only served to bear out what I already knew, in that he was a fantastic player, who deserves all the recognition that he has received over the years.

THE OPPOSITION

The following is a list of players who I didn't get to play alongside, but at some point or other I came into contact with as an opposition player. They are all players that I admired and felt were tough opponents and I would have loved to have played alongside them.

However as a largely one club man, it was never going to happen unless we managed to sign them for Ipswich Town.

(Goal-keeper) Pat Jennings

Pat had the perfect build for a goalkeeper, in that he was a tall, well built guy with hands like coal shovels. For someone so big, he was also very agile and especially good at getting down to make saves from low shots. He was also a very commanding figure and had an immense presence about him whenever you saw him on the pitch. Although he was not one for shouting and bawling, I am sure it was very reassuring to be a defender and know that if someone got past you they still had big Pat to beat.

(Right-back) Tommy Smith

Tommy is a renowned tough-guy and of course known as one of the all time hard-men of football. This obviously made him a very tough competitor and the sort of guy you wanted on your team. Tommy did a very steady job and kept things nice and easy and whenever you faced him you knew that you were going to have a battle on your hands for the full ninety minutes. Not too many people talk about Tommy's abilities as a footballer, which is strange as he was a better player than people gave him credit for. He made 637 appearances for Liverpool and as far as I'm concerned, you don't manage to achieve that by just being a hard-man.

(Left-back) Alan Kennedy

I think that Alan was an extremely underrated player and he was very unlucky to only win two caps for England. He was a superbly fit player, who seemed to be able to get up and down the pitch all afternoon and was equally comfortable going forward as he was on defensive duties. I like full-backs who can get forward, as they can often make things happen at the opposite end of the pitch and Alan was able to do that, not least when he slammed in a superb goal to win the European Cup for Liverpool against Real Madrid.

(Centre-back) Bobby Moore

Bobby was coming to the latter stages of his career when I played against him but you could see that he was still a class act. Bobby read the game so well and had a knack of knowing where he should be. He was a natural leader and had an aura about him that marked him out as special. Unfortunately the nearest I got to playing alongside him was whilst shooting the 'Escape to Victory' scenes. I only wish that I could have played alongside in a 'proper' team as I would have loved to have played with him. I believe that playing alongside Bobby we would have taken care of any two strikers that you'd care to mention. He was a legend – simple as that.

(Centre-back) David O'Leary

David was a very classy performer, who was comfortable on the ball and who could play a lovely brand of football. I played against him when he was only a youngster and I was very impressed at how mature he seemed. Nothing seemed to upset him and he seemed to turn in very assured performances week in and week out. People often speak of Alan Hansen and Mark Lawrenson as the best central defensive partnership that they have seen and whilst I think that they were very good, I think that without sounding arrogant David and myself would have been better.

(Right-midfield) Bobby Charlton

Bobby was in the twilight of his career when I played against him, but like Bobby Moore you could still see the touches of brilliance. I was never overawed, or thought too much about things on a football pitch, but you know that you are doing well when you are lining up against someone like Bobby Charlton. When he told me after my debut that he was impressed with my performance, I took it as the ultimate compliment, as he was quite simply one of the best football players the game has ever seen.

(Centre-midfield) Graeme Souness

Graeme was someone who could play football, but was also happy to accommodate anyone who fancied their chances in a battle. He was very much a leader and the type of player that you wanted to have on your side when it was time to put the tin hats on. Graeme wasn't all about battling though, he was a fine football player, who could get forward and chip in with a few goals here and there. He was the driving force of a fantastic Liverpool side and I would have loved to have played football alongside him as he was a simply magnificent player.

(Centre-midfield) Liam Brady

Liam was a bit like Arnold Muhren in that he was a very graceful, elegant player, with the sweetest left-foot who made the game look easy. I remember when I played in the FA Cup final against Arsenal, that Liam was very much the danger man and someone we would have to keep quiet. Fortunately by his own high standards he didn't have one of his best games and all I can say to that is thank you Liam, as if he had been at the top of his game, we would have had a real job on our hands to deal with him.

(Left-midfield) George Best

What else can you say about George? Everyone already knows that he was an absolute genius and one of the greatest football players of all time. I nearly got to fulfil a lifelong ambition to play alongside George when he played in a testimonial game for the 'Boss' at Portman Road. The sides were made up of an international select eleven featuring George, who played against an England international team. I was thrilled when I was asked to play, but when I was told that I was playing for England, it was the only time that I didn't want to pull on the famous white jersey, as it meant that I was missing out on the chance to line alongside George. An amazing player and a lovely man – George is one of the all time greats.

(Centre-forward) Peter Osgood

Peter was one of my boyhood heroes and I used to imagine that I was him when I was playing on the park pitches and street corners near my home when I was a youngster. It was therefore a bit strange when a few years later I was marking him in a game of top-flight football. Not only was Peter a terrific player with a great eye for goal, he was also a gentleman. A lot of players who played in those days tried to put you off your stride by trying to intimidate you, or come at you with a cheap shot, but not Peter. He wasn't there to get himself involved in anything untoward, he was there to play football, which incidentally was something he was very good at doing.

(Centre-forward) Kenny Dalglish

Kenny was a class act who had everything, he could make a goal from nothing either for himself or a team-mate and he was a very dangerous player to have to play against. Kenny had a tough act to follow as when he went to Liverpool he was following in the footsteps of Kevin Keegan. It is a credit to Kenny, that a player as good as Kevin wasn't really missed. After George Best, I would rate Kenny as the best player that I played against – he really was that good.

***

So there you have it, despite my ultimate misfortune with injuries I still got to line up alongside and against some fantastic footballers. I count myself lucky to have done so and feel blessed to have been part of such a wonderful and beautiful game as football.

KEVIN BEATTIE – PLAYING RECORD

ENGLAND
29/11/1972 – 26/1/1975
Under-23 Appearances 9, Goals 1.
16/4 /1975 – 12/10/1977
Full Appearances 9, Goals 1.

IPSWICH TOWN
1972/73 Appearances 48 (1 as sub), Goals 5.
1973/74 Appearances 57, Goals 6.
1974/75 Appearances 52, Goals 6.
1975/76 Appearances 36, Goals 4.
1976/77 Appearances 33, (1 as sub), Goals 5.
1977/78 Appearances 21, Goals 0.
1978/79 Appearances 26 (1 as sub), Goals 2
1979/80 Appearances 12 (2 as sub), Goals 2.
1980/81 Appearances 11 (6 as sub), Goals 2.
Total Appearances 296 (11 as sub), Goals 32.

COLCHESTER UNITED
1982 Appearances 3 (1 as sub), Goals 0.

MIDDLESBROUGH
1982 Appearances 3 (1 as sub), Goals 1.

Also played for: Barnet, Harwich and Parkeston, Sandvikens (Sweden), Kongsberg (Norway), Nybergsund (Norway).